200
SLOW COOKER
RECIPES

HAMLYN **ALL COLOUR COOKBOOK**

200
SLOW COOKER
RECIPES

SARA LEWIS

An Hachette UK Company
www.hachette.co.uk

First published in Great Britain in 2009 by Hamlyn,
a division of Octopus Publishing Group Ltd,
Carmelite House, 50 Victoria Embankment,
London EC4Y 0DZ
www.octopusbooks.co.uk

This edition published in 2016

ISBN 978-0-600-63349-5

A CIP catalogue record for this book is available
from the British Library

Printed and bound in China

10 9 8 7 6

Standard level spoon measurement are used in all recipes.
1 tablespoon = one 15 ml spoon
1 teaspoon = one 5 ml spoon

Both imperial and metric measures have been given in all
recipes. Use one set of measurements only and not a mixture
of both.

Eggs should be medium unless otherwise stated. The
Department of Health advises that eggs should not be
consumed raw. This book contains dishes made with raw or
lightly cooked eggs. It is prudent for more vulnerable people
such as pregnant and nursing mothers, invalids, the elderly,
babies and young children to avoid uncooked or lightly cooked
dishes made with eggs. Once prepared these dishes should be
kept refrigerated and used promptly.

Fresh herbs should be used unless otherwise stated.

A few recipes contain nuts and nut derivatives. Anyone with a
known nut allergy must avoid these.

Read your slow cooker manual before you begin
and preheat the slow cooker if required according to
the manufacturer's instructions. Because slow cookers
vary slightly from manufacturer to manufacturer, check
recipe timings with the manufacturer's directions
for a recipe using the same ingredients.

All recipes for this book were tested in oval-shaped slow
cookers with a working capacity of 2.5 litres (4 pints) and total
capacity of 3.5 litres (6 pints) using metric measurements.
Where the slow cooker recipe is finished off under the grill, hold
the pot with teacloths to remove it from the machine housing.

contents

introduction

introduction

If you want to prepare healthy, homely meals but feel you just don't have time, then think again. As little as 15–20 minutes spent early in the day are all that are needed to prepare supper to go into a slow cooker, leaving you free to get on with something else.

The slow cooker is ideal for anyone who has a young family because the supper can be put on after the morning school run so that it is ready when you and the children are at your most tired at around half past five in the afternoon. If you work shifts or if you are a student, with lectures during the day, you can put on a meal before you go out so that supper is waiting when you get back. If you are new to retirement, supper can be left to cook while you enjoy a relaxing day at the golf course, or your slow cooker can leave you with the free time to tackle that DIY project you've been putting off.

Because the food cooks so slowly there is no need to worry about it boiling dry, spilling over or burning on the bottom, and depending on the setting it can be left for 8–10 hours. Food that has been slowly cooked has much more flavour than dishes prepared in other ways. When microwave ovens first came into use they captured everyone's imagination as the answer to our busy working lives. And, yes, a microwave oven allows you to cook food in minutes, but the reality is that the food is often tasteless and lacking in colour.

Prepared chilled meals can be reheated in minutes, but they are expensive and somewhat lacking nutritionally.

A slow cooker is environmentally friendly, too. There is no need to turn on the oven for just one dish when you can save fuel by using your slow cooker. It uses around the same amount of electricity as an electric light bulb, so they are cheap to run. In addition, the long, slow cooking transforms even the toughest and cheapest cuts of meat into dishes that melt in the mouth, and the meat quite literally falls off the bone – try for example, Slow-braised Pork with Ratatouille (pages 74–75) or Maple-glazed Ribs (pages 90–91).

Slow cookers are perfect for steaming puddings, too. Because there is no evaporation you won't have to remember to top up the water or return to find that the pot has boiled dry.

When water is added to the pot it can also be used as a bain marie or water bath to cook baked custards, pâtés or terrines. You can pour alcoholic or fruit juice mixtures into the pot and make warming hot party punches or hot toddies.

The slow cooker pot can also be used to make chocolate or cheese fondues, preserves such as lemon curd or simple chutneys, and you can even boil up bones or a chicken carcass to make into homemade stock.

size matters

Slow cookers are available in three sizes and are measured in capacity. The size usually printed on the packaging is the working capacity or the maximum space for food:

- For two people use a mini oval slow cooker with a maximum capacity of 1.5 litres (2½ pints) and a working capacity of 1 litre (1¾ pints).
- For four people choose a round or the more versatile oval cooker with a total capacity of 3.5 litres (6 pints) and a working capacity of 2.5 litres (4 pints).
- For 6 people you will need a large oval slow cooker with a total capacity of 5 litres (8¾ pints) and a working capacity of 4 litres (7 pints) or the extra large round 6.5 litres (11½ pints) with a working capacity of 4.5 litres (8 pints).

Surprisingly, the very large slow cookers cost only a little more than the medium-sized ones, and it is easy to be swept along thinking that they are better value for money. However, unless you have a large family or like to cook large quantities so that you have enough supper for one meal with extra portions to freeze, you will probably find that they are too big for your everyday needs. Remember that you need to half-fill a slow cooker when you are cooking meat, fish or vegetable dishes.

The best and most versatile shape for a slow cooker is an oval, which is ideal for cooking a whole chicken and has ample room for a pudding basin or four individual pudding moulds and yet is capacious enough to make soup for six portions. Choose one with an indicator light so that you can see at a glance when the slow cooker is turned on.

before you start

It is important to read the handbook before using your slow cooker. Some manufacturers recommend preheating the slow cooker on the high setting for a minimum of 20 minutes before food is added. Others recommend that it is heated only when filled with food.

how full should the pot be?

A slow cooker pot must only be used with the addition of liquid – ideally it should be no less than half full. Aim for the three-quarter full mark or, if you are making soups, make sure the liquid is no higher than 2.5 cm (1 inch) from the top.

Joints of meat should take up no more than two-thirds of the space. If you are using a pudding basin, ensure there is 1.5 cm (¾ inch) space all the way round or 1 cm (½ inch) at the narrowest point if using an oval cooker.

heat settings

All slow cookers have a 'high', 'low' and 'off' setting, and some also have either 'medium', 'warm' or 'auto' settings. In general, the 'high' setting will take only half the time of the 'low' setting when you are cooking a diced meat or vegetable casserole. This can be useful if you plan to eat at lunchtime or are delayed in starting the casserole. Both settings will reach just below 100°C (212°F), boiling point, during cooking, but when it is set to 'high' the temperature is reached more quickly.

A combination of settings can be useful and is recommended by some manufacturers at the beginning of cooking. See your manufacturer's handbook for more details.

what is best at what setting?

Following is a general guide to what you should cook at which temperature.

low
• Diced meat or vegetable casseroles
• Chops or chicken joints
• Soups
• Egg custard desserts
• Rice dishes
• Fish dishes

high
• Sweet or savoury steamed puddings or sweet dishes that include a raising agent (either self-raising flour or baking powder).
• Pâtés or terrines.
• Whole chicken, guinea fowl or pheasant, gammon joint or half a shoulder of lamb.

10

timings

All the recipes in the book have variable timings, which means that they will be tender and ready to eat at the lower time but can be left without spoiling for an extra hour or two, which is perfect if you get delayed at work or stuck in traffic.

If you want to speed up or slow down casseroles based on diced meat or vegetables so that the cooking fits around your plans better, adjust the heat settings and timings as suggested below:

Low	Medium	High
6–8 hours	4–6 hours	3–4 hours
8–10 hours	6–8 hours	5–6 hours
10–12 hours	8–10 hours	7–8 hours

(The above timings were taken from the Morphy Richards slow cooker instruction manual. Note: do not change timings or settings for fish, whole joints or dairy dishes.)

using your slow cooker for the first time

Before you start to use the slow cooker, put it on the work surface, somewhere out of the way and make sure that the flex is tucked around the back of the machine and not trailing over the front of the work surface.

The outside of the slow cooker does get hot, so warn young members of the family

and don't forget to wear oven gloves or use tea towels when you are lifting the pot out of the housing. Set it on to a heatproof mat on the table or work surface to serve the food.

If your slow cooker lid has a vent in the top, make sure that the slow cooker is not put under an eye-level cupboard or the steam may catch someone's arm as they reach into the cupboard.

Always check that the joint, pudding basin, soufflé dish or individual moulds will fit into your slow cooker pot before you begin work on a recipe to avoid frustration when you get to a critical point.

preparing food for the slow cooker

meat
Cut meat into pieces that are the same size so that cooking is even, and fry off meat before adding to the slow cooker.

A whole guinea fowl or pheasant, a small gammon joint or half a shoulder of lamb can be cooked in an oval slow cooker pot, but make sure that it does not fill more than the

---

tip

As the slow cooker heats up, it forms a water seal just under the lid, but whenever you lift the lid you break the seal. For each time you lift the lid, add 20 minutes to the cooking time.

lower two-thirds of the pot. Cover it with boiling liquid and cook on high. Check it is cooked either by using a meat thermometer or by inserting a skewer through the thickest part and checking that the juices run clear.

Add boiling stock or sauce to the slow cooker pot and press the meat beneath the surface before cooking begins.

vegetables
Root vegetables can (surprisingly) take longer to cook than meat. If you are adding vegetables to a meat casserole, make sure you cut them into pieces that are a little smaller than the meat and try to keep all the vegetable chunks the same size so that they cook evenly. Press the vegetables and the meat below the surface of the liquid before cooking begins.

When you are making soup, purée it while it is still in the slow cooker pot by using an electric stick blender if you have one.

fish
Whether you cut the fish into pieces or cook it in a larger piece of about 500 g (1 lb), the slow, gentle cooking will not cause the fish to break up or overcook. Make sure that the fish is covered by the hot liquid so that it cooks evenly right through to the centre.

Do not add shellfish until the last 15 minutes of cooking, and make sure that the slow cooker is set to high. If the fish was frozen it must be thoroughly thawed, rinsed with cold water and drained before use.

---

tip
You can make so much more than just a casserole in the slow cooker. Try soups, steamed puddings, baked custards, hot toddies and even cakes, chutneys and preserves.

---

pasta

For best results cook the pasta separately in a saucepan of boiling water and then mix with the casserole just before serving. Small pasta shapes, such as macaroni or shells, can be added to soups 30–45 minutes before the end of cooking.

Pasta can be soaked in boiling water for short-cook recipes, such as Macaroni with Smoked Haddock (see pages 132–3).

rice

Easy-cook rice is preferable for slow cookers because it has been partially cooked during manufacture and some of the starch has been washed off, making it less sticky.

When you are cooking rice, allow a minimum of 250 ml (8 fl oz) water for each 100 g (3½ oz) of easy-cook rice or up to 500 ml (17 fl oz) for risotto rice.

dried pulses

Make sure that you soak dried pulses in plenty of cold water overnight. Drain them, then put them into a saucepan with fresh water and bring to the boil. Boil rapidly for 10 minutes, then drain or add with the cooking liquid to the slow cooker. See the recipes for details.

Pearl barley, lentils — red, Puy or green — do not need soaking overnight. If you are unsure, check the instructions on the packet.

cream and milk

Both cream and milk are generally added at the beginning of cooking only when you are making rice pudding or baked egg custard-style dishes. Use full-fat milk where milk is cooked directly in the cooker pot rather than pudding moulds as it is less likely to separate.

If you are making soup, add the milk at the very end, after the soup has been puréed. Stir cream into soups just 15 minutes before the end of cooking.

thickening stews and casseroles

Casseroles can be thickened in just the same way as if you were cooking conventionally. You can do it either before slow cooking, by adding the flour after searing meat or frying onions, or you can thicken the casserole with cornflour mixed with a little water 30–60 minutes before the end of cooking.

adapting your own recipes

If you have a favourite recipe that you would like to make in your slow cooker, look at a similar recipe in this book to give you an idea of the quantity that will fit into the slow cooker pot and the appropriate timing for the main ingredient. Because a slow cooker cooks food so gently and evenly you will find that you need to reduce the amount of liquid. Begin by using just half the amount of hot liquid, and then add to it as needed, pressing foods beneath the surface of the liquid and increasing the amount until just covered. Recipes that contain fresh tomatoes will turn to pulp during cooking, so you will not need quite so much liquid.

In the slow cooker the steam condenses on the lid and returns to the pot, so there is no danger of recipes boiling dry. If you find

> **tip**
> Whether or not you brown the ingredients first, make sure you always add **hot** liquid to the cooker pot.

you have reduced the amount of liquid too much, add a little more boiling stock or water at the end of cooking to compensate.

It is usually best to add milk or cream at the end of the recipe unless the recipe uses the slow cooker pot as a bain marie or water bath, when hot water is poured around a cooking dish. Rice pudding and porridge is the exception to this, and you should use UHT or full-fat milk and not semi-skimmed or skimmed milk for these. Refer to individual recipes in the book for guidance.

When you are adapting a recipe remember:
• Foods cooked in a slow cooker must contain some liquid.
• Foods will not brown during cooking, so fry off foods before they go in or brown the top by transferring the slow cooker pot from its housing to the grill just before serving or by using a cook's blowtorch.

changing recipes to suit a different model

All the recipes in this book have been tested in a standard sized slow cooker with a total capacity of 3.5 litres (6 pints). You might have a larger 5 litre (8¾ pint) six-portion sized

cooker or a tiny 1.5 litre (2½ pint) two-portion cooker, and to adapt the recipes in this book you can simply halve for two portions or add half as much again to the recipe for more portions, keeping the timings the same. All those recipes made in a pudding basin, soufflé dish or individual moulds may also be cooked in a larger slow cooker for the same amount of time.

for the freezer

The majority of soups and stews in this book can be frozen successfully, and if you have do not have a large family or if you live on your own, freezing individual portions for another meal can be a great time saver. After all, it requires only a little extra effort to make a casserole for four than it does to make one for two. Defrost portions in the fridge overnight or at room temperature for 4 hours,

then reheat thoroughly in a saucepan on the hob or in the microwave on full power.

If you are using raw frozen foods make sure that they are thoroughly thawed before you add them to the slow cooker. Exceptions to this rule are frozen peas and sweetcorn. Raw food that was frozen and is then thawed and cooked in the slow cooker can be refrozen in its cooked and cooled state.

caring for your slow cooker

If you look after it carefully you may find that your machine lasts for 20 years or more.

Because the heat of a slow cooker is so controllable it is not like a saucepan with burned-on grime to contend with. Simply lift the slow cooker pot out of the housing, fill it with hot soapy water and leave to soak for a while. Although it is tempting to pop the slow cooker pot and lid into the dishwasher, they do take up a lot of space, and check with your manual first, because not all are dishwasher proof.

Allow the machine itself to cool down before cleaning. Turn it off at the controls and pull out the plug. Wipe the inside with a damp dish cloth, removing any stubborn marks with a little cream cleaner. The outside of the machine and the controls can be wiped with a dish cloth, then buffed up with a duster or, if it has a chrome-effect finish, sprayed with a little multi-surface cleaner and polished with a duster. **Never immerse the machine in water to clean it.** If you are storing the slow cooker in a cupboard, make sure it is completely cold before you put it away.

---

tip

So that you can easily lift a hot basin out of the slow cooker, tear off two long pieces of foil. Fold each into thirds to make a long, thin strap. Put one on top of the other to make a cross, then sit the pudding basin in the centre. Lift up the straps, then lower the basin into the slow cooker pot carefully. Alternatively, you can buy macramé string pudding basin bags, but do make sure that they will comfortably hold a 1.25 litre (2¼ pint) basin before you buy one.

breakfasts & light bites

banana & cinnamon porridge

Preparation time **5 minutes**
Cooking temperature **low**
Cooking time **1–2 hours**
Serves **4**

600 ml (1 pint) boiling **water**
300 ml (½ pint) **UHT milk**
150 g (5 oz) **porridge oats**
2 **bananas**
4 tablespoons **light** or **dark muscovado sugar**
¼ teaspoon **ground cinnamon**

Preheat the slow cooker if necessary; see the manufacturer's instructions. Pour the boiling water and milk into the slow cooker pot, then stir in the oats.

Cover with the lid and cook on low for 1 hour for 'runny' porridge or 2 hours for 'thick' porridge.

Spoon into bowls, slice the bananas and divide among the bowls. Mix together the sugar and cinnamon and sprinkle over the top.

For hot spiced muesli, follow the recipe as above, adding 175 g (6 oz) Swiss-style muesli. When cooked, stir in ¼ teaspoon ground cinnamon and top with 100 g (3½ oz) diced ready-to-eat dried apricots. Drizzle over 2 tablespoons honey before serving.

eggs en cocotte with salmon

Preparation time **10 minutes**
Cooking temperature **high**
Cooking time **40–45 minutes**
Serves **4**

25 g (1 oz) **butter**
4 **eggs**
4 tablespoons **double cream**
2 teaspoons chopped **chives**
1 teaspoon chopped **tarragon**
200 g (7 oz) **smoked salmon**,
  sliced
salt and **pepper**
4 **lemon wedges**, to garnish
4 slices **toast**, to serve

Preheat the slow cooker if necessary; see the manufacturer's instructions. Liberally butter the inside of 4 heatproof china ramekin dishes, each 150 ml (¼ pint), and break an egg into each ramekin.

Drizzle the cream over the eggs and sprinkle over the herbs and a little salt and pepper. Transfer the ramekins to the slow cooker pot and pour boiling water into the pot to come halfway up the sides of the ramekins.

Cover with the lid (there is no need to cover the dishes with foil) and cook on high for 40–45 minutes or until the egg whites are set and the yolks still slightly soft.

Lift the dishes carefully out of the slow cooker pot with a tea towel, transfer to plates and serve with smoked salmon, lemon wedges and triangles of toast.

For spiced eggs en cocotte, break the eggs into buttered dishes and drizzle over each 1 tablespoon double cream, a few drops of Tabasco sauce and a little salt and pepper. Sprinkle 3 teaspoons finely chopped coriander over the dishes and bake as above. Serve with toast and thin slices of pastrami.

easy sausage & beans

Preparation time **15 minutes**
Cooking temperature **low**
Cooking time **9–10 hours** or
   overnight
Serves **4**

1 tablespoon **sunflower oil**
1 **onion**, chopped
½ teaspoon **smoked paprika**
   (pimenton)
2 × 410 g (13½ oz) cans
   baked beans
2 teaspoons **wholegrain
   mustard**
2 tablespoons **Worcestershire
   sauce**
6 tablespoons **vegetable
   stock**
2 **tomatoes**, roughly chopped
½ **red pepper**, cored,
   deseeded and diced
350 g (11½ oz) chilled
   frankfurters, thickly sliced
salt and **pepper**
buttered **toast**, to serve

Preheat the slow cooker if necessary; see the manufacturer's instructions. Heat the oil in a frying pan, add the onion and fry, stirring, for 5 minutes or until softened and just beginning to turn golden.

Stir in the paprika and cook for 1 minute, then mix in the beans, mustard, Worcestershire sauce and stock. Bring to the boil, then stir in the tomatoes, red pepper and a little salt and pepper.

Add the frankfurters to the slow cooker pot and tip the baked bean mixture over the top. Cover with the lid and cook on low for 9–10 hours or overnight.

Stir well, then spoon into shallow bowls and serve with buttered toast fingers.

For chillied sausage & beans, add ½ teaspoon crushed dried red chillies, ¼ teaspoon cumin seeds, roughly crushed in a pestle and mortar, and a pinch of ground cinnamon to the smoked paprika and fried onion. Omit the mustard and Worcestershire sauce, then continue as above, adding the beans, stock, tomatoes, red pepper and frankfurters. Cook on low for 9–10 hours.

vanilla breakfast prunes & figs

Preparation time **5 minutes**
Cooking temperature **low**
Cooking time **8–10 hours** or
  overnight
Serves **4**

1 **breakfast tea** teabag
600 ml (1 pint) boiling **water**
150 g (5 oz) pitted **prunes**
150 g (5 oz) dried **figs**
75 g (3 oz) **caster sugar**
1 teaspoon **vanilla extract**
pared rind of ½ **orange**

To serve
natural **yogurt**
muesli

Preheat the slow cooker if necessary; see the manufacturer's instructions. Put the teabag into a jug or teapot, add the boiling water and leave to soak for 2–3 minutes. Remove the teabag and pour the tea into the slow cooker pot.

Add the whole prunes and figs, the sugar and vanilla extract to the hot tea, sprinkle with the orange rind and mix together. Cover with the lid and cook on low for 8–10 hours or overnight.

Serve hot with spoonfuls of natural yogurt and a sprinkling of muesli.

For breakfast apricots in orange, put 300 g (10 oz) dried apricots, 50 g (2 oz) caster sugar, 300 ml (½ pint) boiling water and 150 ml (¼ pint) orange juice in the slow cooker pot. Cover and cook as above.

big breakfast bonanza

Preparation time **20 minutes**
Cooking temperature **low**
Cooking time **9–10 hours** or
  overnight
Serves **4**

1 tablespoon **sunflower oil**
12 **herby chipolata**
  sausages, about 400 g
  (13 oz) in total
1 **onion**, thinly sliced
500 g (1 lb) **potatoes**, peeled
  and cut into 2.5 cm (1 inch)
  chunks
375 g (12 oz) **tomatoes**,
  roughly chopped
125 g (4 oz) **black pudding**,
  peeled and cut into chunks
250 ml (8 fl oz) **vegetable**
  stock
2 tablespoons **Worcestershire**
  sauce
1 teaspoon **English mustard**
2–3 stems of **thyme**, plus
  extra to garnish
salt and **pepper**

To serve
slices of **white bread**
  (optional)
4 poached **eggs** (optional)

Preheat the slow cooker if necessary; see the manufacturer's instructions. Heat the oil in a frying pan, add the sausages and brown on one side, turn and add the onion. Fry, turning the sausages and stirring the onions until the sausages are browned but not cooked.

Add the potatoes, tomatoes and black pudding to the slow cooker pot. Lift the sausages and onion from the pan with a slotted spoon and transfer to the slow cooker pot. Pour off the excess fat, then add the stock, Worcestershire sauce and mustard. Tear the leaves from the thyme stems and add to pan with some salt and pepper.

Bring to the boil and pour over the sausages. Press the potatoes down so that the liquid covers them. Cover with the lid and cook on low for 9–10 hours or overnight. Stir before serving and garnish with extra thyme leaves. Serve with slices of white bread or a poached egg.

For a vegetarian big breakfast, fry 400 g (13 oz) meat-free sausages in the oil with the onion as above. Add the potatoes and tomatoes to the slow cooker pot with 125 g (4 oz) halved button mushrooms instead of the black pudding. Heat the stock with the mustard and thyme and add 1 tablespoon tomato purée instead of the Worcestershire sauce. Season with salt and pepper, then pour the mixture over the sausages in the slow cooker. Cover and cook as above.

cajun red bean soup

Preparation time **25 minutes**, plus overnight soaking
Cooking temperature **low**
Cooking time **8½–10½ hours**
Serves **6**

125 g (4 oz) **dried red kidney beans**, soaked overnight in cold water
2 tablespoons **sunflower oil**
1 large **onion**, chopped
1 **red pepper**, cored, deseeded and diced
1 **carrot**, diced
1 **baking potato**, diced
2–3 **garlic cloves**, chopped (optional)
2 teaspoons mixed **Cajun spice** or ½–1 teaspoon **chilli powder**
400 g (13 oz) can **chopped tomatoes**
1 tablespoon **brown sugar**
1 litre (1¾ pints) hot **vegetable stock**
50 g (2 oz) **okra**, sliced
50 g (2 oz) **green beans**, cut into short lengths
salt and **pepper**

Preheat the slow cooker if necessary; see the manufacturer's instructions. Drain and rinse the soaked beans, add to a saucepan, cover with fresh water and bring to the boil. Boil vigorously for 10 minutes, then drain into a sieve.

Meanwhile, heat the oil in a large frying pan. Add the onion and fry, stirring, for 5 minutes or until softened. Add the red pepper, carrot, potato and garlic (if used) and fry for 2–3 minutes. Stir in the Cajun spice, tomatoes, sugar and plenty of salt and pepper and bring to the boil.

Transfer the mixture to the slow cooker pot, add the drained beans and hot stock and mix together. Cover with the lid and cook on low for 8–10 hours.

Add the green vegetables, replace the lid and cook for 30 minutes. Ladle the soup into bowls and serve with crusty bread, if liked.

For Hungarian paprika & red bean soup, make up the soup as above but add 1 teaspoon smoked paprika instead of the Cajun spice. Cook as above, omitting the green vegetables. Purée, return to the slow cooker and top up with a little boiling water if needed. Ladle into soup bowls, top each with 2 tablespoons soured cream and a few caraway seeds and serve.

chilli black bean stew

Preparation time **30 minutes**, plus overnight soaking
Cooking temperature **low**
Cooking time **8–10 hours**
Serves **4–6**

250 g (8 oz) **dried black beans**, soaked overnight in cold water
2 tablespoons **olive oil**
1 large **onion**, chopped
2 **carrots**, diced
2 **celery sticks**, sliced
2–3 **garlic cloves**, chopped
1 teaspoon **fennel seeds**, crushed
1 teaspoon **cumin seeds**, crushed
2 teaspoons **coriander seeds**, crushed
1 teaspoon **chilli powder** or **smoked paprika** (pimenton)
400 g (13 oz) can **chopped tomatoes**
300 ml (½ pint) **vegetable stock**
1 tablespoon **brown sugar**
150 g (5 oz) **soured cream** or **natural yogurt** (optional)
salt and **pepper**
boiled **rice** or crusty **bread**, to serve

Preheat the slow cooker if necessary; see the manufacturer's instructions. Drain and rinse the soaked beans. Place them in a saucepan, add fresh water to cover and bring to the boil. Boil vigorously for 10 minutes, then drain into a sieve.

Meanwhile, heat the oil in a saucepan, add the onion and fry, stirring, for 5 minutes or until softened. Add the carrots, celery and garlic and fry for 2–3 minutes. Stir the crushed fennel, cumin and coriander seeds into the vegetables with the chilli powder and cook for 1 minute.

Add the tomatoes, stock, sugar and a little pepper. Bring to the boil, then pour into the slow cooker pot. Mix in the beans, pressing them under the liquid, then cover with the lid and cook on low for 8–10 hours.

Season the cooked beans to taste with salt. Top with spoonfuls of soured cream or yogurt and avocado salsa (see below) and serve accompanied by boiled rice or crusty bread.

For avocado salsa to accompany the stew halve an avocado and remove the stone and skin. Dice the flesh, and toss with the grated rind and juice of 1 lime. Mix with ½ finely chopped red onion, 2 diced tomatoes and 2 tablespoons chopped coriander leaves. Make the salsa about 10 minutes before serving the stew.

chicken & noodle broth

Preparation time **10 minutes**
Cooking temperature **high**
Cooking time **5 hours**
20 minutes–7½ hours
Serves **4**

1 **chicken** carcass
1 **onion**, cut into wedges
2 **carrots**, sliced
2 **celery sticks**, sliced
1 **bouquet garni**
1.25 litres (2¼ pints) boiling
water
75 g (3 oz) **vermicelli pasta**
4 tablespoons chopped
parsley
salt and **pepper**

Preheat the slow cooker if necessary; see the manufacturer's instructions. Put the chicken carcass into the slow cooker pot, breaking it into 2 pieces if necessary to make it fit. Add the onion, carrots, celery and bouquet garni.

Pour over the boiling water and add a little salt and pepper. Cover with the lid and cook on high for 5–7 hours.

Strain the soup into a large sieve, then quickly pour the hot soup back into the slow cooker pot. Take any meat off the carcass and add to the pot. Taste and adjust the seasoning if needed. Add the pasta and cook on high for 20–30 minutes or until the pasta is just cooked. Sprinkle with parsley and ladle into deep bowls. Serve with warm bread, if liked.

For chicken & minted pea soup, make up the soup base as above, then strain and pour it back into the slow cooker. Add 200 g (7 oz) finely sliced leeks, 375 g (12 oz) frozen peas and a small bunch of mint, cover and cook on high for 30 minutes. Mash or purée with a stick blender, then stir in 150 g (5 oz) mascarpone cheese until melted. Ladle into bowls and sprinkle with extra mint leaves, if liked.

smoked salmon timbales

Preparation time **30 minutes**, plus chilling
Cooking temperature **low**
Cooking time **3–3½ hours**
Serves **4**

butter for greasing
200 ml (7 fl oz) **full-fat crème fraîche**
4 **egg yolks**
grated rind and juice of ½ **lemon**
1 small growing pot of **basil**
100 g (3 ½ oz) sliced **smoked salmon**
salt and **pepper**
lemon wedges, to garnish

Preheat the slow cooker if necessary; see the manufacturer's instructions. Lightly butter 4 individual metal moulds, each 150 ml (¼ pint), and base-line with circles of nonstick baking or greaseproof paper.

Put the crème fraîche in a bowl and gradually beat in the egg yolks. Add the lemon rind and juice and season with salt and pepper. Chop half of the basil and 75 g (3 oz) of the smoked salmon, then stir both into the crème fraîche mixture.

Pour the mixture into the prepared moulds. Stand the moulds in the slow cooker pot (there is no need to cover them with foil). Pour hot water around the moulds to come halfway up the sides, cover with the lid and cook on low for 3–3½ hours or until the moulds are set.

Remove the moulds carefully from the slow cooker using a tea towel and leave to cool at room temperature. Transfer to the refrigerator and chill for at least 4 hours or overnight.

Loosen the edges of the timbales with a knife dipped in hot water, then invert on to serving plates and remove the moulds. Smooth any rough areas with the side of the knife and remove the lining discs. Top with the remaining smoked salmon and basil leaves and garnish with lemon wedges.

For smoked mackerel timbales, omit the basil and smoked salmon and stir in 3 tablespoons freshly chopped chives, ½ teaspoon hot horseradish and 75 g (3 oz) skinned, flaked smoked mackerel fillets. Continue as above. Serve with salad.

gingered sweet potato soup

Preparation time **30 minutes**
Cooking temperature **low and high**
Cooking time **6¼–8¼ hours**
Serves **6**

1 tablespoon **olive oil**
1 **onion**, chopped
2 **garlic cloves**, finely chopped
1 teaspoon **fennel seeds**, crushed
4 cm (1½ inch) **fresh root ginger**, peeled and finely chopped
900 ml (1½ pints) **vegetable stock**
500 g (1 lb) **sweet potatoes**, diced
150 g (5 oz) **red lentils**
300 ml (½ pint) **full-fat milk**
salt and **pepper**
warm **naan bread**, to serve

To garnish
2 tablespoons **olive oil**
1 **onion**, thinly sliced
1 teaspoon **fennel seeds**, crushed
½ teaspoon **ground cumin**
¼ teaspoon **ground turmeric**
1 teaspoon **caster sugar**

Preheat the slow cooker if necessary; see the manufacturer's instructions. Heat the oil in a large frying pan, add the onion and fry, stirring, for 5 minutes or until lightly browned. Add the garlic, fennel seeds and ginger and cook for 2 minutes. Add the stock and salt and pepper and bring to the boil.

Put the sweet potatoes and lentils in the slow cooker pot, pour over the hot stock mixture, cover with the lid and cook on low for 6–8 hours or until the potatoes and lentils are soft.

Purée the soup, in batches if necessary, and return it to the slow cooker. Stir in the milk and cook on high for 15 minutes.

Meanwhile, make the garnish. Heat the oil in a clean frying pan, add the onion and fry over a low heat, stirring occasionally, for 10 minutes or until softened. Stir in the spices and sugar, increase the heat slightly and fry for 5 more minutes or until golden brown.

Ladle the soup into bowls and sprinkle the spicy onions over the top. Serve with warm naan bread.

For curried red lentil & carrot soup, fry the onion and garlic in oil as above. Omit the seeds and ginger and instead add 4 teaspoons balti curry paste (or a curry paste of your choice). Cook for 2 minutes, then mix in vegetable stock and lentils, adding 500 g (1 lb) diced carrots instead of the sweet potatoes. Continue as above, serving with a swirl of yogurt instead of the fried onion mix.

potato, apple & bacon hotpot

Preparation time **20 minutes**
Cooking temperature **low**
Cooking time **9–10 hours** or
  overnight
Serves **4**

750 g (1½ lb) **potatoes**, thinly
  sliced
25 g (1 oz) **butter**
1 tablespoon **sunflower oil**
2 **onions**, roughly chopped
250 g (8 oz) **smoked back
  bacon**, diced
1 **dessert apple**, cored and
  sliced
2 tablespoons **plain flour**
450 ml (¾ pint) **chicken stock**
2 teaspoons **English mustard**
2 **bay leaves**
50 g (2 oz) **Cheddar cheese**,
  grated
salt and **pepper**

Preheat the slow cooker if necessary; see the manufacturer's instructions. Bring a large saucepan of water to the boil, add the potatoes and cook for 3 minutes, then drain.

Heat the butter and oil in a frying pan, add the onions and bacon and fry, stirring, for 5 minutes or until just beginning to turn golden. Stir in the apple and flour and season the mixture well.

Layer the potatoes and the onion mixture alternately in the slow cooker pot, ending with a layer of potatoes. Bring the stock and mustard to the boil in the frying pan, then pour into the slow cooker pot and add the bay leaves. Cover with the lid and cook on low for 9–10 hours.

Sprinkle the top of the potatoes with the cheese, lift the pot out of the housing using oven gloves and brown under the grill, if liked, then spoon into shallow bowls. Serve with grilled tomato halves sprinkled with chopped chives, if liked.

For cidered chicken & bacon hotpot, blanch the potatoes as above, then fry the onions with 125 g (4 oz) diced smoked back bacon and 4 diced boneless and skinless chicken thighs. Stir in the apple, flour and seasoning, then layer in the slow cooker pot with the potatoes. Heat 300 ml (½ pint) chicken stock, 150 ml (¼ pint) dry cider and the mustard and continue as above. Serve as a supper dish.

caldo verde

Preparation time **20 minutes**

Cooking temperature **low** and **high**

Cooking time **6¼ hours–8 hours 20 minutes**

Serves **6**

2 tablespoons **olive oil**

2 **onions**, chopped

2 **garlic cloves**, finely chopped

150 g (5 oz) **chorizo** in one piece, skinned and diced

625 g (1¼ lb) or 3 small **baking potatoes**, cut into 1 cm (½ inch) dice

1 teaspoon **smoked paprika** (pimenton)

1.2 litres (2 pints) hot **chicken stock**

125 g (4 oz) **green cabbage**, finely shredded

salt and **pepper**

Preheat the slow cooker if necessary; see the manufacturer's instructions. Heat the oil in a large frying pan, add the onions and fry, stirring, for 5 minutes or until lightly browned. Add the garlic, chorizo, potatoes and paprika and cook for 2 minutes.

Transfer the mixture to the slow cooker pot, add the hot stock and season to taste with salt and pepper. Cover with the lid and cook on low for 6–8 hours.

Add the cabbage, replace the lid and cook on high for 15–20 minutes or until the cabbage is tender. Ladle the soup into bowls and serve with warm, crusty bread, if liked.

For caldo verde with pumpkin, prepare the soup as above, reducing the baking potatoes to 375 g (12 oz) and adding 250 g (8 oz) peeled, deseeded and diced pumpkin. Reduce the chicken stock to 900 ml (1½ pints) and add a 400 g (13 oz) can chopped tomatoes.

beery cheese fondue

Preparation time **15 minutes**
Cooking temperature **high**
Cooking time **40–60 minutes**
Serves **4**

15 g (½ oz) **butter**
2 **shallots** or ½ small **onion**,
  finely chopped
1 **garlic clove**, finely chopped
3 teaspoons **cornflour**
200 ml (7 fl oz) **blonde beer**
  or **lager**
200 g (7 oz) **Gruyère cheese**
  (rind removed), grated
175 g (6 oz) **Emmental**
  cheese (rind removed),
  grated
grated **nutmeg**
salt and **pepper**

To serve
½ wholewheat **French stick**,
  cubed
2 **celery sticks**, cut into short
  lengths
8 small **pickled onions**,
  drained and halved
1 bunch of **radishes**, tops
  trimmed
1 **red pepper**, cored,
  deseeded and cubed
2 **endives**, leaves separated

Preheat the slow cooker if necessary; see the manufacturer's instructions. Butter the inside of the slow cooker pot, then add the shallots or onion and garlic.

Put the cornflour in a small bowl and mix with a little of the beer to make a smooth paste, then blend with the remaining beer. Add to the slow cooker with both cheeses, a little nutmeg and some salt and pepper.

Stir together, then cover with the lid and cook on high for 40–60 minutes, whisking once during cooking. Whisk again and serve with the dippers arranged on a serving plate, with long fondue or ordinary forks for dunking the dippers into the fondue.

For classic cheese fondue, omit the beer from the above ingredients and add 175 ml (6 fl oz) dry white wine and 1 tablespoon Kirsch. Cook as above and serve with bread to dip.

chunky chickpea & chorizo soup

Preparation time **20 minutes**
Cooking temperature **low**
Cooking time **6–8 hours**
Serves **4**

2 tablespoons **olive oil**
1 **onion**, chopped
2 **garlic cloves**, finely
   chopped
150 g (5 oz) **chorizo**, skinned
   and diced
¾ teaspoon **smoked paprika**
   (pimenton)
2–3 stems **thyme**
1 litre (1¾ pint) **chicken stock**
1 tablespoon **tomato purée**
375 g (12 oz) **sweet**
   potatoes, diced
410 g (13½ oz) can
   chickpeas, drained
salt and **pepper**
chopped **parsley** or extra
   thyme leaves, to garnish

Preheat the slow cooker if necessary; see the manufacturer's instructions. Heat the oil in a frying pan, add the onion and fry, stirring, for 5 minutes or until just beginning to turn golden.

Stir in the garlic and chorizo and cook for 2 minutes. Mix in the paprika, add the thyme, stock and tomato purée and bring to the boil, stirring, then add a little salt and pepper.

Add the sweet potatoes and chickpeas to the slow cooker pot and pour over the hot stock mixture. Cover with the lid and cook on low for 6–8 hours until the sweet potatoes are tender.

Ladle into bowls, sprinkle with a little chopped parsley or extra thyme and serve with warm pitta breads, if liked.

For tomato, chickpea & chorizo soup, make the soup as above up to the point where the paprika and thyme have been added. Reduce the stock to 750 ml (1¼ pints) and add to the frying pan with the tomato purée and 2 teaspoons brown sugar. Bring to the boil. Omit the sweet potatoes but add 500 g (1 lb) skinned and diced tomatoes to the slow cooker pot along with the chickpeas. Pour over the stock mixture and continue as above.

brandied duck & walnut terrine

Preparation time **45 minutes**,
plus overnight chilling
Cooking temperature **high**
Cooking time **5–6 hours**
Serves **6**

175 g (6 oz) rindless **smoked
streaky bacon** rashers
1 tablespoon **olive oil**
1 **onion**, chopped
2 boneless **spare rib pork
chops**, about 275 g (9 oz)
in total
2 boneless **duck breasts**,
about 375 g (12 oz) in total,
fat removed
2 **garlic cloves**, chopped
3 tablespoons **brandy**
75 g (3 oz) **fresh
breadcrumbs**
50 g (2 oz) **sun-dried
tomatoes** in oil, drained and
chopped
3 **pickled walnuts**, drained
and roughly chopped
1 **egg**, beaten
1 tablespoon **green
peppercorns**, roughly
crushed
salt

Preheat the slow cooker if necessary; see the manufacturer's instructions. Lay the bacon rashers on a chopping board and stretch each one, using the flat of a large cook's knife, until half as long again. Line the base and sides of a 15 cm (6 inch) diameter, deep heatproof soufflé dish with bacon.

Heat the oil in a frying pan, add the onion and fry, stirring, for 5 minutes. Finely chop or mince the pork and 1 of the duck breasts. Cut the second duck breast into long, thin slices and set aside. Stir the garlic and minced or chopped meat into the pan and cook for 3 minutes. Add the brandy, flame with a match and stand well back until the flames subside.

Stir in the remaining ingredients. Mix well, then press half the mixture into the bacon-lined dish. Top with the sliced duck, then add the remaining mixture. Fold the bacon ends over the top, adding any leftover rashers to cover the gaps. Cover with foil.

Place the dish on an upturned saucer in the base of the slow cooker pot. Pour boiling water around the dish to come halfway up the sides. Cover with the lid and cook on high for 5–6 hours or until the meat juices run clear when the centre of the terrine is pierced with a knife.

Lift the dish carefully out of the pot using a tea towel, stand on a plate, remove the foil top and replace with greaseproof paper. Weigh down the top of the terrine with measuring weights set on a small plate. Transfer to the refrigerator when cool enough and chill overnight.

Loosen the edge of the terrine with a knife, turn out, cut into thick slices and serve.

carrot, orange & fennel soup

Preparation time **25 minutes**
Cooking temperature **low**
Cooking time **6¼–8¼ hours**
Serves **4**

25 g (1 oz) **butter**
1 tablespoon **sunflower oil**
1 large **onion**, chopped
1 teaspoon **fennel seeds**,
   roughly crushed
625 g (1¼ lb) **carrots**, diced
grated rind and juice of
   1 orange
1 litre (1¾ pints) **vegetable
   stock**
salt and **pepper**

To serve
8 tablespoons **double cream**
handful of **croutons**

Preheat the slow cooker if necessary; see the manufacturer's instructions. Heat the butter and oil in a frying pan, add the onion and fry, stirring, for 5 minutes or until the onion is just beginning to soften.

Stir in the fennel seeds and cook for 1 minute to release the flavour. Mix in the carrots, fry for 2 more minutes, then stir in the orange rind and juice. Tip into the slow cooker pot. Bring the stock to the boil in the frying pan, add salt and pepper, then pour into the slow cooker pot. Cover with the lid and cook on low for 6–8 hours or until the carrots are tender.

Transfer to a liquidizer and purée, in batches if necessary, until smooth, then return to the slow cooker pot. Alternatively, purée the soup still in the slow cooker pot with a stick blender. Reheat if necessary in the covered slow cooker pot for 15 minutes.

Ladle the soup into bowls and serve with drizzled cream and croutons.

For Moroccan-spiced carrot soup, prepare the soup as above, replacing the fennel seeds with 1 teaspoon cumin seeds and 1 teaspoon coriander seeds, both crushed, and ½ teaspoon of smoked paprika and ½ teaspoon of turmeric. Omit the orange rind and juice and add 150 ml (¼ pint) milk or milk and double cream mixed before reheating.

meat, poultry & game

lamb shanks with juniper

Preparation time **15 minutes**
Cooking temperature **high**
Cooking time **5–7 hours**
Serves **4**

25 g (1 oz) **butter**
4 **lamb shanks**, about 1.5 kg
  (3 lb) in total
2 small **red onions**, cut into
  wedges
2 tablespoons **plain flour**
200 ml (7 fl oz) **red wine**
450 ml (¾ pint) **lamb stock**
2 tablespoons **cranberry
  sauce** (optional)
1 tablespoon **tomato purée**
2 **bay leaves**
1 teaspoon **juniper berries**,
  roughly crushed
1 small **cinnamon stick**,
  halved
pared rind of 1 small **orange**
salt and **pepper**

To serve
mashed **sweet potatoes**
green beans

Preheat the slow cooker if necessary; see the manufacturer's instructions. Heat the butter in a frying pan, add the lamb shanks and fry over a medium heat, turning until browned all over. Drain and put into the slow cooker pot.

Add the onions to the pan and fry for 4–5 minutes or until just beginning to turn golden. Stir in the flour. Gradually mix in the wine and stock, then add the cranberry sauce (if used) and the remaining ingredients. Bring to the boil, stirring.

Transfer to the slow cooker pot, cover with the lid and cook on high for 5–7 hours or until the lamb is beginning to fall off the bone. If you prefer a thick sauce, pour it into a saucepan and boil rapidly for 5 minutes or until reduced by one-third. Serve the lamb with mashed sweet potatoes and green beans.

For lamb shanks with lemon, fry the lamb shanks as above, then fry 2 sliced white onions. Mix with the flour and add 200 ml (7 fl oz) dry white wine, the lamb stock, 4 teaspoons roughly crushed coriander seeds, the bay leaves, the pared rind of 1 lemon and 2 teaspoons honey. Season and bring to the boil, pour over the lamb and cook as above.

thai green chicken curry

Preparation time **20 minutes**
Cooking temperature **low** and **high**
Cooking time **8¼–10¼ hours**
Serves **4**

1 tablespoon **sunflower oil**
2 tablespoons **Thai green curry paste**
2 teaspoons **galangal paste**
2 Thai **green chillies**, deseeded and thinly sliced
1 **onion**, finely chopped
8 **chicken thighs**, about 1 kg (2 lb) in total, skinned, boned and cubed
400 ml (14 fl oz) **full-fat coconut milk**
150 ml (¼ pint) **chicken stock**
4 dried **kaffir lime leaves**
2 teaspoons **light muscovado sugar**
2 teaspoons **fish sauce**
100 g (3½ oz) **sugar snap peas**
100 g (3½ oz) **green beans**, cut in half
small bunch of **coriander**

Preheat the slow cooker if necessary; see the manufacturer's instructions. Heat the oil in a frying pan, add the curry paste, galangal paste and green chillies and cook for 1 minute.

Stir in the onion and chicken and cook, stirring, until the chicken is just beginning to turn golden. Pour in the coconut milk and stock, then add the lime leaves, sugar and fish sauce. Bring to the boil, stirring.

Transfer the mixture into the slow cooker pot, cover with the lid and cook on low for 8–10 hours or until the chicken is tender.

Stir in the peas and beans and cook on high for 15 minutes or until they are just tender. Tear the coriander leaves over the top, then spoon into bowls and serve with rice.

For Thai red chicken curry, make up the curry as above but omit the green curry paste and green chillies and instead add 2 tablespoons red curry paste and 2 finely chopped garlic cloves. Cook for 8–10 hours as above but do not add the peas and beans, then spoon into bowls and sprinkle with some torn coriander leaves.

pork, orange & star anise

Preparation time **20 minutes**
Cooking temperature **low**
Cooking time **8–10 hours**
Serves **4**

1 tablespoon **sunflower oil**
4 **pork shoulder steaks** or
  boneless **spare rib chops**,
  about 700 g (1 lb 7 oz) in
  total, each cut into 3
1 **onion**, chopped
2 tablespoons **plain flour**
450 ml (¾ pint) **chicken stock**
grated rind and juice of
  1 orange
3 tablespoons **plum sauce**
2 tablespoons **soy sauce**
3–4 whole **star anise**
1 fresh or dried **red chilli**,
  halved (optional)
salt and **pepper**
grated rind of **1 orange**
mashed **potatoes** mixed with
  steamed **green vegetables**,
  to serve

Preheat the slow cooker if necessary; see the
manufacturer's instructions. Heat the oil in a large
frying pan, add the pieces of pork and fry over a high
heat until browned on both sides. Lift the pork out of
the pan with a slotted spoon and transfer to a plate.

Add the onion to the pan and fry, stirring, for 5 minutes
or until lightly browned. Stir in the flour, then mix in the
stock, orange rind and juice, plum sauce, soy sauce,
star anise and chilli (if used). Season with salt and
pepper and bring to the boil, stirring.

Transfer the pork to the slow cooker pot and pour
the sauce over it. Cover with the lid and cook on low
for 8–10 hours. Sprinkle with grated orange rind and
serve with mashed potatoes mixed with steamed
green vegetables.

For pork, orange & bay leaves, prepare the dish as
above, but replace the plum sauce, soy sauce, star
anise and red chilli with 2 bay leaves, 2 teaspoons light
muscovado sugar and 1 tablespoon balsamic vinegar.

creamy tarragon chicken

Preparation time **15 minutes**
Cooking temperature **high**
Cooking time **3–4 hours**
Serves **4**

1 tablespoon **olive oil**
15 g (½ oz) **butter**
4 boneless, skinless **chicken breasts**, about 650 g (1 lb 6 oz) in total
200 g (7 oz) **shallots**, halved
1 tablespoon **plain flour**
300 ml (½ pint) **chicken stock**
4 tablespoons **dry vermouth**
2 sprigs of **tarragon**, plus extra to serve
3 tablespoons **double cream**
2 tablespoons chopped **chives**
salt and **pepper**
coarsely mashed **potatoes** mixed with **peas**, to serve

Preheat the slow cooker if necessary; see the manufacturer's instructions. Heat the oil and butter in a frying pan, add the chicken and fry over a high heat until golden on both sides but not cooked through. Drain and put into the slow cooker pot in a single layer.

Add the shallots to the frying pan and cook, stirring, for 4–5 minutes or until just beginning to turn golden. Stir in the flour, then gradually mix in the stock and vermouth. Add the sprigs of tarragon, a little salt and pepper and bring to the boil, stirring.

Pour the sauce over the chicken breasts, cover with the lid and cook on high for 3–4 hours or until the chicken is cooked through to the centre.

Stir the cream into the sauce and sprinkle the chicken with 1 tablespoon chopped tarragon and the chives. Serve with coarsely mashed potatoes mixed with peas.

For creamy pesto chicken, prepare the dish as above, but replace the vermouth with 4 tablespoons white wine and the tarragon with 1 tablespoon pesto. Sprinkle the chicken with some tiny basil leaves and a little grated Parmesan cheese instead of the chives. Serve the chicken sliced, if liked, and mixed with cooked penne pasta and drizzled with the creamy sauce.

chillied beef with cheesy tortillas

Preparation time **20 minutes**
Cooking temperature **low**
Cooking time **8–10 hours**
Serves **4**

1 tablespoon **sunflower oil**
500 g (1 lb) extra lean **minced beef**
1 **onion**, chopped
2 **garlic cloves**, finely chopped
1 teaspoon **smoked paprika**
½ teaspoon crushed dried **red chillies**
1 teaspoon **ground cumin**
1 tablespoon **plain flour**
400 g (13 oz) can **chopped tomatoes**
410 g (13½ oz) can **red kidney beans**, drained
150 ml (¼ pint) **beef stock**
1 tablespoon **dark muscovado sugar**
salt and **pepper**

Topping
100 g (3½ oz) **tortilla chips**
½ **red pepper**, cored, deseeded and diced
chopped **coriander**
100 g (3½ oz) mature **Cheddar cheese**, grated

Preheat the slow cooker if necessary; see the manufacturer's instructions. Heat the oil in a frying pan, add the mince and onion and fry, stirring, for 5 minutes, breaking up the mince with a spoon until it is browned.

Stir in the garlic, paprika, chillies and cumin and cook for 2 minutes. Stir in the flour. Mix in the tomatoes, kidney beans, stock and sugar, season with salt and pepper and pour the mixture into the slow cooker pot. Cover with the lid and cook on low for 8–10 hours.

Stir the chilli, then arrange the tortilla chips on top. Sprinkle over the remaining ingredients, lift the pot out of the housing using oven gloves and brown under a hot grill until the cheese just melts. Spoon into bowls to serve.

For turkey fajitas with guacamole, make up the chilli as above, using 500 g (1 lb) minced turkey instead of the beef. To serve, halve, stone and peel 1 avocado and mash the flesh with the juice of 1 lime, a small bunch of torn fresh coriander and some salt and pepper. Spoon the turkey mixture on to 8 warmed, medium soft flour tortillas, top with spoonfuls of guacamole and 8 tablespoons soured cream, if liked, and roll up to serve.

cidered pork with sage dumplings

Preparation time **25 minutes**
Cooking temperature **low**
Cooking time **9–11 hours**
Serves **4**

1 tablespoon **sunflower oil**
750 g (1½ lb) **pork shoulder steaks**, cubed and any fat discarded
1 **leek**, thinly sliced: the green and white parts kept separate
2 tablespoons **plain flour**
300 ml (½ pint) **dry cider**
300 ml (½ pint) **chicken stock**
200 g (7 oz) **carrot**, diced
1 **dessert apple**, cored and diced
2–3 stems of **sage**
salt and **pepper**

Dumplings
150 g (5 oz) **self-raising flour**
75 g (3 oz) **vegetable suet**
1 tablespoon chopped **sage**
2 tablespoons chopped **parsley**
5–7 tablespoons **water**

Preheat the slow cooker if necessary; see the manufacturer's instructions. Heat the oil in a frying pan, add the pork a few pieces at a time until all the pieces are in the pan, then fry over a high heat until lightly browned. Lift out of pan with a slotted spoon and transfer to the slow cooker pot.

Add the white leek slices to the pan and fry for 2–3 minutes or until softened. Stir in the flour, then gradually mix in the cider and stock. Add the carrot, apple, sage and some salt and pepper. Bring to the boil, stirring. Pour the mixture into the slow cooker pot, cover with the lid and cook on low for 8–10 hours or until the pork is tender.

Make the dumplings. Put the flour, suet, herbs and a little salt and pepper into a bowl, mix together, then gradually stir in enough water to make a soft but not sticky dough. Cut into 12 pieces and roll into balls with floured hands. Stir the green leek slices into the pork casserole and arrange the dumplings on the top. Cover and cook, still on low, for 1 hour until they are well risen. Spoon into shallow bowls to serve.

For beery pork with rosemary dumplings, make up the casserole as above, adding 300 ml (½ pint) blonde beer or lager instead of the cider and 300 g (10 oz) mixed diced parsnip, carrot and swede instead of the carrots and apple. Flavour with 2 stems of rosemary instead of the sage and add 1 tablespoon chopped rosemary instead of sage to the dumplings.

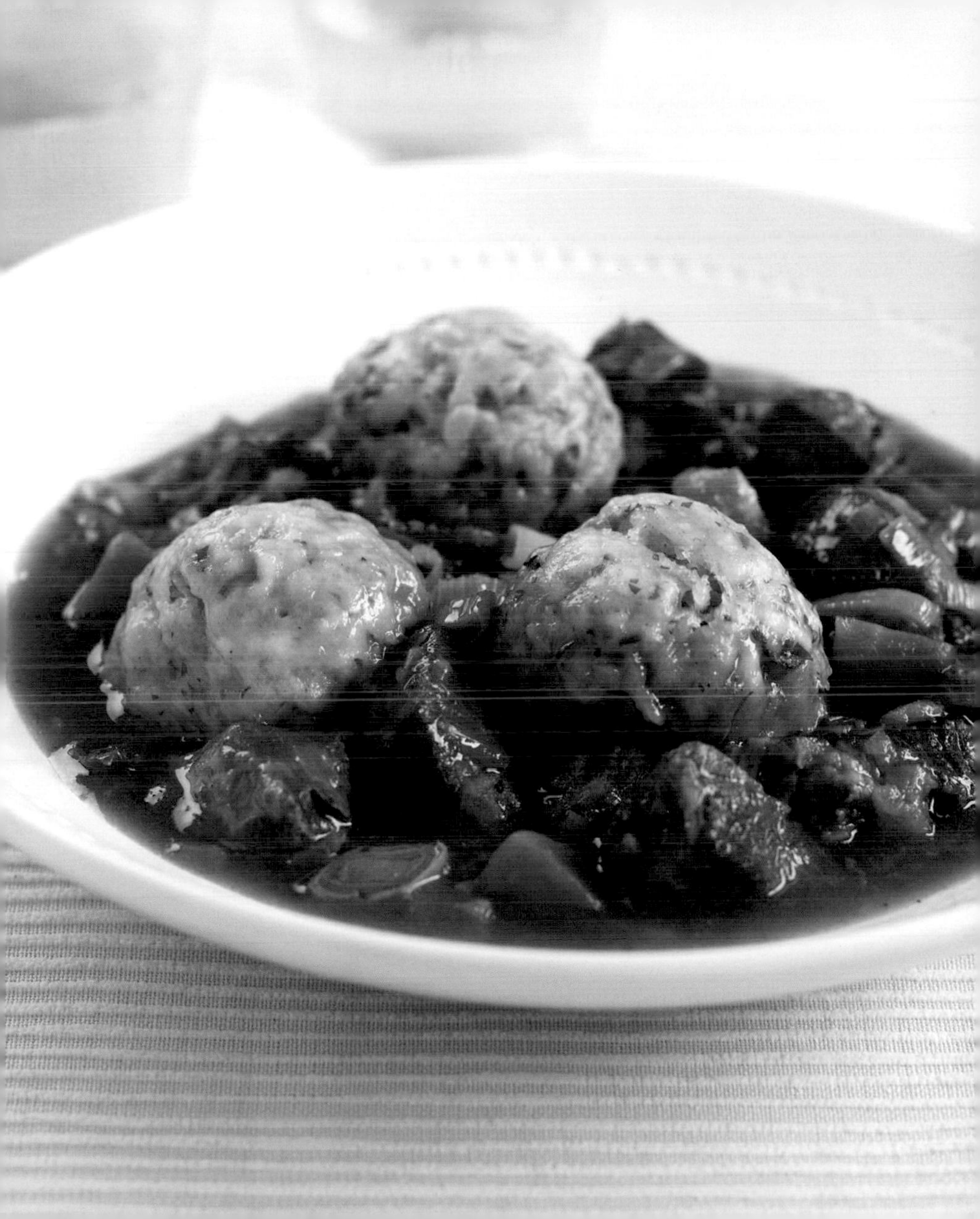

kashmiri butter chicken

Preparation time **30 minutes**
Cooking temperature **low**
Cooking time **5–7 hours**
Serves **4**

2 **onions**, quartered
3 **garlic cloves**
4 cm (1½ inch) **fresh root ginger**, peeled
1 large **red chilli**, deseeded
8 boneless, skinless **chicken thighs**
1 tablespoon **sunflower oil**
25 g (1 oz) **butter**
1 teaspoon **cumin seeds**, crushed
1 teaspoon **fennel seeds**, crushed
4 **cardamom pods**, crushed
1 teaspoon **paprika**
1 teaspoon **ground turmeric**
¼ teaspoon **ground cinnamon**
300 ml (½ pint) **chicken stock**
1 tablespoon **brown sugar**
2 tablespoons **tomato purée**
5 tablespoons **double cream**
salt

To garnish
toasted flaked almonds
sprigs of **coriander**

Preheat the slow cooker if necessary; see the manufacturer's instructions. Blend the onions, garlic, ginger and chilli in a food processor or liquidizer or chop finely.

Cut each chicken thigh into 4 pieces. Heat the oil in a large frying pan and add the chicken a few pieces at a time until all the meat has been added. Cook over a high heat until browned. Drain and transfer to a plate.

Add the butter to the frying pan. When it has melted, add the onion paste and cook over a more moderate heat until it is just beginning to colour. Stir in the cumin and fennel seeds, cardamom pods and ground spices. Cook for 1 minute, then mix in the stock, sugar, tomato purée and salt. Bring to the boil, stirring.

Transfer the chicken to the slow cooker pot, pour the onion mixture and sauce over the top and press the pieces of chicken below the surface of the liquid. Cover with the lid and cook on low for 5–7 hours.

Stir in the cream. Garnish with toasted flaked almonds and sprigs of coriander and serve with plain boiled rice.

For coriander flat breads to accompany the curry, mix together 200 g (7 oz) self-raising flour, ½ teaspoon baking powder, 3 tablespoons roughly chopped coriander leaves and a little salt in a bowl. Add 2 tablespoons sunflower oil, then gradually mix in 6–7 tablespoons water to make a soft dough. Cut the dough into 4 pieces and roll out each piece thinly on a lightly floured surface to form a rough oval. Cook on a preheated ridged frying pan for 3–4 minutes on each side until singed and puffy.

red cooked chinese duck

Preparation time **20 minutes**
Cooking temperature **high**
Cooking time **5–6 hours**
Serves **4**

4 **duck legs**, each about
   200 g (7 oz)
1 **onion**, sliced
2 tablespoons **plain flour**
450 ml (¾ pint) **chicken stock**
2 tablespoons **soy sauce**
1 tablespoon **red wine
   vinegar**
1 tablespoon **clear honey**
2 teaspoons **tomato purée**
2 teaspoons **fish sauce**
½ teaspoon crushed dried **red
   chillies**
½ teaspoon **ground allspice**
4 **star anise**
375 g (12 oz) **red plums**,
   stoned and quartered
rice or **gingered noodles**,
   to serve

Preheat the slow cooker if necessary; see the manufacturer's instructions. Dry-fry the duck legs in a frying pan over a low heat at first until the fat begins to run, then increase the heat and brown on both sides. Lift out of the pan with a slotted spoon and transfer to the slow cooker pot.

Pour off all but 1 tablespoon of the duck fat from the pan, then add the onion and fry, stirring, for 5 minutes or until just turning golden. Stir in the flour, then gradually mix in the stock. Add the remaining ingredients, except for the plums, and bring to the boil, stirring.

Pour the sauce over the duck, add the plums and press the duck beneath the surface of the liquid. Cover with the lid and cook on high for 5–6 hours or until the duck is almost falling off the bones. Serve with rice or with gingered noodles (see below).

For gingered noodles to accompany the duck, heat 1 tablespoon sesame oil in a wok, add 2.5 cm (1 inch) piece peeled and finely chopped fresh root ginger, 200 g (7 oz) finely shredded pak choi, 50 g (2 oz) halved mangetout and 3 packs, each 150 g (5 oz), of thick-cut, straight-to-wok noodles. Stir-fry for 3–4 minutes or until the pak choi has just wilted and the noodles are hot.

baked ham in cola

Preparation time **15 minutes**
Cooking temperature **high**
Cooking time **6–7 hours**
Serves **4**

1.25 kg (2½ lb) boneless
smoked gammon joint,
soaked overnight in cold
water
5 **cloves**
1 **onion**, cut into 8 wedges
2 **carrots**, thickly sliced
410 g (13½ oz) can **black
beans** or **red kidney beans**,
drained
2 **bay leaves**
900 ml (1½ pints) **cola**
1 tablespoon **dark
muscovado sugar**
1 tablespoon **tomato purée**
2 teaspoons **English mustard**

Preheat the slow cooker if necessary; see the manufacturer's instructions. Drain the gammon joint and put it into the slow cooker pot. Press the cloves into 5 of the onion wedges and add with the remaining onion wedges and carrot slices to the gammon. Tip in the drained beans and add the bay leaves.

Pour the cola into a saucepan, add the sugar, tomato purée and mustard and bring to the boil, stirring. Pour over the gammon, cover with the lid and cook on high for 6–7 hours or until the gammon is tender.

Strain the cooking liquid into a saucepan and boil rapidly for 10 minutes to reduce by half. Keep the gammon and vegetables hot in the turned-off slow cooker with the lid on.

Slice the gammon thinly and arrange on plates with the vegetables, beans and a drizzle of sauce. Serve with baked potatoes and broccoli, if liked.

For baked ham with parsley sauce, soak the gammon as above and cook in the slow cooker pot with the cloves, onion, carrots, bay leaves and 900 ml (1½ pints) boiling water instead of the cola. Omit the beans and remaining ingredients. Melt 25 g (1 oz) butter in a saucepan for the parsley sauce. Stir in 25 g (1 oz) plain flour, cook for 1 minute then mix in 300 ml (½ pint) milk. Bring to the boil, stirring until thickened and smooth. Stir in 1 teaspoon English mustard, 3 tablespoons chopped parsley and salt and pepper. Serve with the sliced gammon and drained onion and carrots.

lamb rogan josh

Preparation time **15 minutes**
Cooking temperature **low**
Cooking time **8–10 hours**
Serves **4**

25 g (1 oz) **butter**
750 g (1½ lb) **lamb fillet**,
  sliced
2 **onions**, chopped
3 **garlic cloves**, finely
  chopped
2.5 cm (1 inch) **fresh root
  ginger**, peeled and finely
  chopped
1 teaspoon **ground turmeric**
2 teaspoons **ground
  coriander**
2 teaspoons **cumin seeds**,
  roughly crushed
2 teaspoons **garam masala**
½ teaspoon crushed dried **red
  chillies**
2 tablespoons **plain flour**
400 g (13 oz) can **chopped
  tomatoes**
300 ml (½ pint) **lamb stock**
4 tablespoons **double cream**

To garnish
small bunch of **coriander**,
  leaves torn
shredded **red onion**

Preheat the slow cooker if necessary; see the manufacturer's instructions. Heat the butter in a frying pan, add the lamb a few pieces at a time until all the meat is in the pan, then fry, stirring, over a high heat until browned. Lift out of the pan with a slotted spoon and add to the slow cooker pot.

Add the onions to the pan and fry, stirring, for 5 minutes or until softened and just beginning to turn golden. Stir in the garlic, ginger, spices and dried chillies and cook for 1 minute. Mix in the flour, then add the tomatoes and stock. Bring to the boil, stirring.

Pour the tomato mixture over the lamb, cover with the lid and cook on low for 8–10 hours or until the lamb is tender. Stir in the cream, garnish with coriander leaves and serve with pilau rice (see below) and naan bread, if liked.

For pilau rice to accompany the curry, rinse 225 g (7½ oz) basmati rice in a sieve several times, drain, then soak in cold water for 15 minutes. Heat 15 g (½ oz) butter in a saucepan, add 1 finely chopped onion and fry for 3 minutes. Add 5 lightly crushed cardamom pods, 5 cloves, ½ cinnamon stick, ½ teaspoon ground turmeric and ½ teaspoon salt. Cook for 1 minute. Drain the rice, add to the pan and cook for 1 minute. Pour in 475 ml (16 fl oz) boiling water, bring back to the boil, cover tightly and simmer gently for 10 minutes. Take the saucepan from the heat but do not remove the lid. Leave to stand for 8–10 minutes. Fluff up with a fork and serve.

beef stew with dumplings

Preparation time **35 minutes**
Cooking temperature **low** and **high**
Cooking time **8–10½ hours**
Serves **4**

2 tablespoons **olive oil**
750 g (1½ lb) **braising beef**, cubed and any fat discarded
1 large **onion**, chopped
2–3 **garlic cloves**, chopped
2 tablespoons **plain flour**
300 ml (½ pint) Burgundy **red wine**
300 ml (½ pint) **beef stock**
1 tablespoon **tomato purée**
2 **bay leaves**
150 g (5 oz) baby **carrots**, larger ones halved
250 g (8 oz) **leeks**, trimmed, cleaned and thinly sliced
salt and **pepper**

Horseradish dumplings
150 g (5 oz) **self-raising flour**
75 g (3 oz) **shredded suet**
2 teaspoons **creamed horseradish**
3 tablespoons snipped **chives**
5–7 tablespoons **water**
salt and **pepper**

Preheat the slow cooker if necessary; see the manufacturer's instructions. Heat the oil in a frying pan and add the beef, a few cubes at a time, until all the pieces have been added to the pan. Fry over a high heat until just beginning to brown, then add the onion and fry, stirring, for 5 minutes.

Stir in the garlic and flour, then gradually mix in the wine and stock. Add the tomato purée and bay leaves and season with salt and pepper. Bring to the boil, then transfer the mixture to the slow cooker pot. Cover with the lid and cook on low for 7–9 hours.

Stir the stew, then add the carrots, replace the lid and cook on high for 30–45 minutes.

Meanwhile, make the dumplings. Mix the flour, suet, horseradish, chives and salt and pepper in a bowl. Stir in enough water to make a soft but not sticky dough. With floured hands, shape into 8 balls.

Stir the leeks into the stew, then add the dumplings, replace the lid and cook for another 30–45 minutes still on high or until the dumplings are light and fluffy. Spoon into shallow dishes and serve, remembering to remove the bay leaves.

For Guinness beef stew with mustard dumplings,
make up the stew as above, replacing the red wine with 300 ml (½ pint) Guinness or stout. Top with dumplings made with 3 teaspoons wholegrain mustard instead of the creamed horeradish and chives.

slow-braised pork with ratatouille

Preparation time **20 minutes**
Cooking temperature **high**
Cooking time **7—9 hours**
Serves **4**

1 tablespoon **olive oil**
1 **onion**, chopped
1 **red pepper**, cored,
   deseeded and cut into
   chunks
1 **yellow pepper**, cored,
   deseeded and cut into
   chunks
375 g (12 oz) **courgettes**, cut
   into chunks
2 **garlic cloves**, finely
   chopped
400 g (13 oz) can **chopped
   tomatoes**
150 ml (¼ pint) **red wine** or
   chicken stock
1 tablespoon **cornflour**
2—3 stems of **rosemary**,
   leaves torn from stems
875 g (1¾ lb) piece thick end
   belly pork, rind and any
   string removed
salt and **pepper**
mashed **potatoes**, to serve

Preheat the slow cooker if necessary; see the manufacturer's instructions. Heat the oil in a frying pan, add the onion and fry, stirring, for 5 minutes or until just beginning to turn golden.

Add the peppers, courgettes and garlic and fry for 2 minutes, then mix in the tomatoes and the wine or stock. Mix the cornflour to a smooth paste with a little water, then stir into the pan with the rosemary leaves and some seasoning. Bring to the boil, stirring.

Tip half the mixture into the slow cooker pot, add the unrolled belly pork and cover with the rest of the vegetable mixture. Cover with the lid and cook on high for 7—9 hours or until the pork is almost falling apart. If you like your sauces thick, ladle it out of the slow cooker pot into a saucepan and boil for 5 minutes to reduce down. Cut the pork into 4 pieces, then spoon into shallow dishes and serve with mashed potatoes and the tomato sauce.

For braised chicken with ratatouille, fry 4 chicken thigh and leg joints in 1 tablespoon olive oil until browned on both sides. Drain and transfer to the slow cooker pot. Make up the ratatouille as above, spoon it over the chicken and cook on high for 5—6 hours.

74

sun-dried tomato & chicken pilaf

Preparation time **25 minutes**
Cooking temperature **high**
Cooking time **3—4 hours**
Serves **4**

1 tablespoon **olive oil**
4 boneless, skinless **chicken breasts**
1 large **onion**, roughly chopped
2 **garlic cloves**, chopped (optional)
400 g (13 oz) can **chopped tomatoes**
50 g (2 oz) **sun-dried tomatoes** in oil, drained and sliced
2 teaspoons **pesto**
600 ml (1 pint) hot **chicken stock**
150 g (5 oz) **easy-cook brown rice**
50 g (2 oz) **wild rice**
salt and **pepper**

To serve
rocket salad
olive oil and **lemon** dressing

Preheat the slow cooker if necessary; see the manufacturer's instructions. Heat the oil in a frying pan and fry the chicken breasts on one side only until browned. Remove from the pan with a slotted spoon and reserve on a plate.

Fry the onion and garlic (if used) in the pan, stirring, for 5 minutes or until lightly browned. Add the tomatoes, sun-dried tomatoes and pesto, season with salt and pepper and bring to the boil. Pour into the slow cooker pot, then stir in the stock.

Rinse the brown rice well in a sieve under cold running water, then stir into the slow cooker pot with the wild rice. Arrange the chicken breasts on top of the rice, browned side up, pressing them just below the level of the liquid so that they don't dry out during cooking. Cover with the lid and cook on high for 3—4 hours or until the chicken is cooked and the rice is tender.

Spoon on to serving plates and serve with a rocket salad tossed in an olive oil and lemon dressing

For red pepper, lemon & chicken pilaf, fry 4 boneless, skinless chicken breasts as above and transfer to a plate. In the pan fry 1 large, roughly chopped onion and 1 cored, deseeded and diced red pepper until the onion is just turning golden. Add 400 g (13 oz) can chopped tomatoes and 2 tablespoons finely chopped lemon thyme leaves and the grated rind and juice of 1 lemon. Bring to the boil, add to the slow cooker with 600 ml (1 pint) hot chicken stock, 150 g (5 oz) easy-cook brown rice and the chicken. Continue as above.

moussaka

Preparation time **30 minutes**
Cooking temperature **low**
Cooking time **8¾–11¼ hours**
Serves **4**

4 tablespoons **olive oil**
1 large **aubergine**, thinly
  sliced
500 g (1 lb) **minced lamb**
1 **onion**, chopped
2 **garlic cloves**, finely
  chopped
1 tablespoon **plain flour**
400 g (13 oz) can **chopped
  tomatoes**
200 ml (7 fl oz) **lamb stock**
1 teaspoon **ground cinnamon**
¼ teaspoon grated **nutmeg**
1 tablespoon **tomato purée**
salt and **pepper**

Topping
3 **eggs**
250 g (8 oz) **natural yogurt**
75 g (3 oz) **feta cheese**,
  grated
pinch of grated **nutmeg**

Preheat the slow cooker if necessary; see the manufacturer's instructions. Heat half the oil in a frying pan and fry the aubergine slices in batches, adding more oil as needed until they have all been fried and are softened and lightly browned on both sides. Drain and transfer to a plate.

Add the minced lamb and onion to the frying pan and dry-fry, stirring and breaking up the lamb, until evenly browned. Stir in the garlic and flour, then mix in the tomatoes, stock, spices, tomato purée and a little salt and pepper. Bring to the boil, stirring.

Spoon the lamb mixture into the slow cooker pot and arrange the aubergine slices on top, overlapping. Cover with the lid and cook on low for 8–10 hours.

Make the custard topping. Mix together the eggs, yogurt, feta, nutmeg and spoon over the top of the aubergine. Replace the lid and cook, still on low, for ¾–1¼ hours or until set. Lift the pot out of the housing using oven gloves and brown under a hot grill. Serve with salad.

For Greek shepherds' pie, prepare the mince, top with the fried aubergine slices and cook as above. Omit the custard topping and instead peel and cut 750 g (1½ lb) potatoes into chunks and cook in a saucepan of boiling water for 15 minutes or until soft. Drain and mash with 3 tablespoons Greek yogurt and some salt and pepper. Lift the pot out of the housing, spoon the mash over the aubergine, dot with 25 g (1 oz) butter and brown under a hot grill.

sausages with onion gravy

Preparation time **15 minutes**
Cooking temperature **low**
Cooking time **6—8 hours**
Serves **4**

1 tablespoon **sunflower oil**
8 'gourmet' flavoured
    sausages, such as **Sicilian**
    or **Toulouse**
2 **red onions**, halved and
    thinly sliced
2 teaspoons **light muscovado**
    sugar
2 tablespoons **plain flour**
450 ml (¾ pint) **beef stock**
1 tablespoons sun-dried or
    ordinary **tomato purée**
1 **bay leaf**
salt and **pepper**

To serve
large **Yorkshire puddings**
steamed **carrots**
steamed **broccoli**

Preheat the slow cooker if necessary; see the manufacturer's instructions. Heat the oil in a frying pan, add the sausages and fry over a high heat for 5 minutes, turning until browned on all sides but not cooked through. Drain and transfer to the slow cooker pot.

Add the onions to the frying pan and fry over a medium heat for 5 minutes or until softened. Add the sugar and fry, stirring, for 5 more minutes or until the onion slices are caramelized around the edges.

Stir in the flour, then gradually mix in the stock. Add the tomato purée, the bay leaf and some salt and pepper and bring to the boil, still stirring. Pour over the sausages. Cover with the lid and cook on low for 6—8 hours or until the sausages are tender.

Serve spooned into reheated ready-made large Yorkshire puddings accompanied with steamed carrots and broccoli or mashed potatoes.

For sausages with beery onion gravy, fry 8 large traditional herb sausages instead of the 'gourmet' ones until browned. Drain, then fry 2 sliced white onions until softened, and omit the sugar. Stir in plain flour, then mix in 150 ml (¼ pint) stout or brown beer and reduce the beef stock to 300 ml (½ pint). Replace the tomato purée with 1 tablespoon wholegrain mustard and 2 tablespoons Worcestershire sauce. Season and bring to the boil. Cook in the slow cooker for 6—8 hours.

pheasant with pancetta

Preparation time **35 minutes**
Cooking temperature **low**
Cooking time **2½–3 hours**
Serves **4**

4 **pheasant breasts**, about
600 g (1 lb 3 oz) in total
small bunch of **sage**
100 g (3½ oz) **smoked
pancetta**, sliced
25 g (1 oz) **butter**
200 g (7 oz) **shallots**, halved
if large
2 tablespoons **plain flour**
150 ml (¼ pint) **dry cider**
150 ml (¼ pint) **chicken stock**
1 teaspoon **Dijon mustard**
1 **dessert apple**, cored and
sliced
240 g (7¾ oz) can whole
peeled **chestnuts**, drained
salt and **pepper**
steamed **baby carrots**,
to serve

Preheat the slow cooker if necessary; see the manufacturer's instructions. Rinse the pheasant breasts with cold water, pat dry with kitchen paper and season well with salt and pepper. Top each breast with a few sage leaves, then wrap in pancetta slices until completely covered. Tie at intervals with fine string to keep the pancetta in place.

Heat the butter in a frying pan, add the shallots and fry for 4–5 minutes or until browned. Stir in the flour, then add the cider, stock and mustard. Add the apple and chestnuts and a little extra salt and pepper. Bring to the boil, stirring.

Arrange the pheasant breasts in the slow cooker pot. Pour the hot onion mixture over the top, cover with the lid and cook on low for 2½–3 hours or until the pheasant is tender and cooked through to the centre. Spoon on to plates, remove the string from the pheasant and serve with baby carrots.

For pheasant with bacon & red wine, add a sage leaf to each pheasant breast, then wrap each one with a stretched rasher of smoked streaky bacon. Fry as above with the shallots until the bacon is browned. Stir in the flour, then add 150 ml (½ pint) red wine in place of the cider, stock and mustard. Omit the apple and instead add 8 halved ready-to-eat prunes and the chestnuts. Cook as above.

sweet & sour chicken

Preparation time **20 minutes**
Cooking temperature **low**
Cooking time **6¼–8¼ hours**
Serves **4**

1 tablespoon **sunflower oil**
8 small **chicken thighs**, about
  1 kg (2 lb) in total, skinned,
  boned and cubed
4 **spring onions**, thickly
  sliced; white and green parts
  kept separate
2 **carrots**, halved lengthways
  and thinly sliced
2.5 cm (1 inch) **fresh root
  ginger**, peeled and finely
  chopped
430 g (14¼ oz) can
  pineapple chunks in natural
  juice
300 ml (½ pint) **chicken stock**
1 tablespoon **cornflour**
1 tablespoon **tomato purée**
2 tablespoons **caster sugar**
2 tablespoons **soy sauce**
2 tablespoons **malt vinegar**
225 g (7½ oz) can **bamboo
  shoots**, drained
125 g (4 oz) **bean sprouts**
100 g (3½ oz) **mangetout**,
  thinly sliced
rice, to serve

Preheat the slow cooker if necessary; see the manufacturer's instructions. Heat the oil in a frying pan, add the chicken thighs and fry, stirring, until browned on all sides. Mix in the white sliced spring onions, carrots and ginger and cook for 2 minutes.

Stir in the pineapple chunks and their juice and the stock. Put the cornflour, tomato purée and sugar into a small bowl, then gradually mix in the soy sauce and vinegar to make a smooth paste. Stir into the frying pan and bring to the boil, stirring.

Tip the chicken and sauce into the slow cooker pot, add the bamboo shoots and press the chicken beneath the surface of the sauce. Cover with the lid and cook on low for 6–8 hours.

When almost ready to serve, add the green spring onion, the beansprouts and mangetout to the slow cooker pot and mix well. Replace the lid and cook, still on low, for 15 minutes or until the vegetables are just tender. Spoon into rice-filled bowls.

For lemon chicken, make up the recipe as above to the addition of the chicken stock. Gradually mix the juice of 1 lemon into the cornflour to make a smooth paste, then stir into the stock with 2 tablespoons dry sherry and 4 teaspoons caster sugar. Bring to the boil, stirring, then add to the slow cooker pot and cook as above, adding the green spring onion, bean sprouts and mangetout at the end.

spiced meatballs with dill sauce

Preparation time **25 minutes**
Cooking temperature **low**
Cooking time **6–8 hours**
Serves **4**

1 **onion**, quartered
50 g (2 oz) **bread**
250 g (8 oz) minced **pork**
250 g (8 oz) minced **beef**
1 teaspoon **ground mixed
  spice**
1 **egg yolk**
1 tablespoon **sunflower oil**
salt and **pepper**
mashed **potato**, to serve

Sauce
15 g (½ oz) **butter**
1 **onion**, sliced
2 tablespoons **plain flour**
600 ml (1 pint) **chicken stock**
4 teaspoons chopped **dill**,
  plus extra to garnish

Preheat the slow cooker if necessary; see the manufacturer's instructions. Finely chop the onion and bread in a food processor or liquidizer. Add the minced meats, mixed spice, egg yolk and a little seasoning and mix together.

Divide the meat mixture into 24 and roll into balls with wetted hands. Heat the oil in a frying pan, add the meatballs and fry over a medium heat, turning until evenly browned but not cooked through. Drain and transfer to the slow cooker pot.

Make the sauce. Add the butter and onion to the cleaned frying pan. Fry, stirring, for 5 minutes or until the onion is softened and just beginning to turn golden. Stir in the flour, then gradually mix in the stock and bring to the boil, stirring. Season and pour the sauce over the meatballs. Cover with the lid and cook on low for 6–8 hours.

Stir the chopped dill into the sauce and serve the meatballs with mashed potato sprinkled with a little extra chopped dill to garnish.

For meatballs in tomato sauce, make up the meatballs as above but omit the mixed spice. For the sauce fry 1 chopped onion in 1 tablespoon olive oil. Add 2 finely chopped garlic cloves, 400 g (13 oz) can chopped tomatoes, 1 teaspoon caster sugar, 150 ml (¼ pint) chicken stock and salt and pepper. Bring to the boil, pour over the meatballs and cook as above. Finish with some torn basil leaves and serve with pasta.

peppered venison with scones

Preparation time **35 minutes**
Cooking temperature **low** and
 high
Cooking time **8¾–11 hours**
Serves **4**

25 g (1 oz) **butter**
1 tablespoon **olive oil**
750 g (1½ lb) **venison
 shoulder**, diced
1 large **red onion**, sliced
125 g (4 oz) **cup
 mushrooms**, sliced
2 **garlic cloves**, chopped
2 tablespoons **plain flour**
200 ml (7 fl oz) **red wine**
250 ml (8 fl oz) **chicken stock**
2 teaspoons **tomato purée**
2 tablespoons **redcurrant jelly**
1 teaspoon **peppercorns**,
 roughly crushed
salt

Scones
250 g (8 oz) **self-raising flour**
40 g (1½ oz) **butter**, diced
125 g (4 oz) **Gorgonzola
 cheese**
3 tablespoons chopped
 parsley or **chives**
1 **egg**, beaten
4–5 tablespoons **milk**

Preheat the slow cooker if necessary; see the manufacturer's instructions. Heat the butter and oil in a large frying pan, add the diced venison a few pieces at time until all the meat has been added, then fry until evenly browned. Transfer to a plate.

Add the onion to the pan and fry for 5 minutes. Stir in the mushrooms, garlic and flour and cook for 1 minute. Stir in the wine, stock, tomato purée, redcurrant jelly, peppercorns and salt and bring to the boil.

Arrange the venison in the slow cooker pot, add the hot wine mixture and press the venison below the surface. Cover with the lid and cook on low for 8–10 hours.

When almost ready to serve, make the scones. Put the flour in a bowl, add the butter and rub in with the fingertips until the mixture resembles fine breadcrumbs. Stir in a little salt and pepper, the cheese and herbs. Reserve 1 tablespoon of egg for glazing and add the rest. Gradually mix in enough milk to make a soft dough.

Knead lightly, then pat the dough into a thick oval or a round that is a little smaller than the top of your slow cooker. Cut it into 8 wedges and arrange, spaced slightly apart, on top of the venison. Cover and cook on high for ¾–1 hour.

Lift the pot out of the housing using oven gloves, brush the scones with the reserved egg and brown under the grill. Serve with green beans, if liked.

maple-glazed ribs

Preparation time **25 minutes**
Cooking temperature **high**
Cooking time **5—7 hours**
Serves **4**

1.25 kg (2½ lb) **pork ribs**,
  rinsed with cold water and
  drained
1 **onion**, quartered
1 **carrot**, thickly sliced
2 **bay leaves**
2 tablespoons **malt vinegar**
1 teaspoon **black**
  peppercorns
½ teaspoon **salt**
1 litre (1¾ pints) boiling **water**

Glaze
2 teaspoons **English mustard**
1 teaspoon **ground allspice**
2 tablespoons **tomato purée**
2 tablespoons **brown sugar**
125 ml (4 fl oz) **maple syrup**

Coleslaw
2 **carrots**, grated
¼ **red cabbage**, shredded
3 **spring onions**, sliced
100 g (3½ oz) **sweetcorn**,
  thawed if frozen
2 tablespoons **mayonnaise**
2 tablespoons **natural yogurt**

Preheat the slow cooker if necessary; see the manufacturer's instructions. Put the pork, onion, carrot, bay leaves, vinegar, peppercorns, salt and water into the slow cooker pot, cover with the lid and cook on high for 5—7 hours or until the ribs are tender.

Lift the ribs out of the slow cooker using a slotted spoon and transfer to a foil-lined grill pan. Mix together the ingredients for the glaze with 150 ml (¼ pint) hot stock from the slow cooker pot. Spoon over the ribs, then grill them for 10—15 minutes, turning once or twice, until browned and sticky.

Meanwhile, mix the ingredients for the coleslaw together and spoon into 4 small bowls. Place these on dinner plates, then pile the ribs on to the plates to serve.

For Chinese ribs, cook the pork ribs in the slow cooker as above. Drain and transfer to a foil-lined grill pan, then glaze with a mixture of 2 tablespoons tomato purée, 2 tablespoons soy sauce, 4 tablespoons hoisin sauce, 2 tablespoons light muscovado sugar, the juice of 1 orange and 150 ml (¼ pint) stock from the slow cooker pot. Grill for 10—15 minutes as above.

gourmet bolognese

Preparation time **20 minutes**
Cooking temperature **low**
Cooking time **8–10 hours**
Serves **4**

1 tablespoon **olive oil**
500 g (1 lb) lean **minced beef**
1 **onion**, chopped
225 g (7½ oz) **chicken livers**,
   thawed if frozen
2 **garlic cloves**, finely
   chopped
50 g (2 oz) **pancetta** or
   smoked back bacon, diced
150 g (5 oz) **cup
   mushrooms**, sliced
1 tablespoon **plain flour**
150 ml (¼ pint) **red wine**
150 ml (¼ pint) **beef stock**
400 g (13 oz) can **chopped
   tomatoes**
2 tablespoons **tomato purée**
1 **bouquet garni**
salt and **pepper**
300 g (10 oz) **tagliatelle**

To serve
shaved **Parmesan cheese**
basil leaves

Preheat the slow cooker if necessary; see the manufacturer's instructions. Heat the oil in a frying pan, add the mince and onion and fry, stirring and breaking up the mince with a spoon until it is evenly browned.

Meanwhile, rinse the chicken livers in a sieve, drain and then chop roughly, discarding any white cores. Add to the frying pan with the garlic, pancetta or bacon and mushrooms and cook for 2–3 minutes or until the livers are browned.

Stir in the flour, then mix in the wine, stock, tomatoes, tomato purée, bouquet garni and seasoning. Bring to the boil, stirring. Spoon into the slow cooker pot, cover with the lid and cook on low for 8–10 hours.

Just before serving, add the tagliatelle to a saucepan of boiling salted water and cook for 8 minutes or until just tender. Drain and stir into the bolognese. Spoon into shallow bowls and sprinkle with Parmesan shavings and some basil leaves.

For budget bolognese, omit the chicken livers and pancetta or bacon and add 1 diced carrot and 1 diced courgette along with the garlic and mushrooms. Replace the wine with extra stock and continue as above.

pot-roasted chicken with lemon

Preparation time **25 minutes**
Cooking temperature **high**
Cooking time **5–6 hours**
Serves **4–5**

1.5 kg (3 lb) whole **chicken**
2 tablespoons **olive oil**
1 large **onion**, cut into
  6 wedges
500 ml (17 fl oz) **dry cider**
3 teaspoons **Dijon mustard**
2 teaspoons **caster sugar**
900 ml (1½ pints) hot **chicken stock**
3 **carrots**, cut into chunks
3 **celery sticks**, thickly sliced
1 **lemon**, cut into 6 wedges
20 g (¾ oz) **tarragon**
3 tablespoons **crème fraîche**
salt and **pepper**

Preheat the slow cooker if necessary; see the manufacturer's instructions. Wash the chicken inside and out with cold water and pat dry with kitchen paper. Heat the oil in a large frying pan, add the chicken, breast side down, and fry for 10 minutes, turning the chicken several times until browned all over.

Put the chicken, breast side down, in the slow cooker pot. Fry the onion wedges in the remaining oil in the pan until lightly browned. Add the cider, mustard and sugar and season with salt and pepper. Bring to the boil, then pour over the chicken. Add the hot stock, then the vegetables, lemon wedges and 3 sprigs of the tarragon, making sure that the chicken and all the vegetables are well below the level of the stock so that they cook evenly and thoroughly.

Cover with the lid and cook on high for 5–6 hours or until the chicken is thoroughly cooked and the meat juices run clear when the thickest parts of the leg and breast are pierced with a sharp knife. Turn the chicken after 4 hours, if liked.

Lift the chicken out of the stock, drain well and transfer to a large serving plate. Remove the vegetables with a slotted spoon and arrange them around the chicken. Measure 600 ml (1 pint) of the hot cooking stock from the slow cooker pot into a jug. Reserve a few sprigs of tarragon to garnish, chop the remainder and whisk into the jug with the crème fraîche to make a gravy. Adjust the seasoning to taste. Carve the chicken in the usual way and serve with the gravy and vegetables. Garnish with lemon wedges, if liked, and the reserved tarragon sprigs, torn into pieces.

beef & root vegetable hotpot

Preparation time **25 minutes**
Cooking temperature **high**
Cooking time **7–8 hours**
Serves **4**

1 tablespoon **sunflower oil**
750 g (1½ lb) **braising beef**,
  cubed
1 **onion**, chopped
2 tablespoons **plain flour**
600 ml (1 pint) **beef stock**
2 tablespoons **Worcestershire sauce**
1 tablespoon **tomato purée**
2 teaspoons **English mustard**
3 sprigs of **rosemary**
125 g (4 oz) **carrots**, diced
125 g (4 oz) **swede**, diced
125 g (4 oz) **parsnip**, diced
700 g (1 lb 6 oz) **potatoes**,
  thinly sliced
25 g (1 oz) **butter**
salt and **pepper**

Preheat the slow cooker if necessary; see the manufacturer's instructions. Heat the oil in a frying pan, add the beef a few pieces at a time until all the meat is in the pan, then fry over a high heat, stirring, until browned. Scoop the beef out of pan with a slotted spoon and transfer to the slow cooker pot.

Add the onion to the pan and fry, stirring, for 5 minutes or until softened and just beginning to turn golden. Stir in the flour, then gradually mix in the stock. Add the Worcestershire sauce, tomato purée, mustard and leaves from 2 sprigs of the rosemary. Season and bring to the boil, stirring.

Add the diced vegetables to the slow cooker pot. Pour the onions and sauce over them, then cover with the potato slices, arranging them so that they overlap and pressing them down into the stock. Sprinkle with the leaves torn from the remaining stem of rosemary and a little salt and pepper.

Cover and cook on high for 7–8 hours until the potatoes are tender. Lift the pot out of the housing using oven gloves, dot the potatoes with the butter and brown under a hot grill, if liked.

For chicken & black pudding hotpot, replace the beef with 625 g (1¼ lb) chicken thighs that have been skinned, boned and diced. Continue as above, adding 100 g (3½ oz) diced black pudding along with the root vegetables. Cover with the potatoes and cook as above.

minted lamb with couscous

Preparation time **25 minutes**
Cooking temperature **high**
Cooking time **7–8 hours**
Serves **4**

1 tablespoon **olive oil**
½ **shoulder** of **lamb**, 900 g–
  1 kg (1 lb 14 oz–2 lb)
1 **onion**, sliced
2 **garlic cloves**, finely
  chopped
2 tablespoons **plain flour**
3 tablespoons **mint jelly**
150 ml (¼ pint) **red wine**
300 ml (½ pint) **lamb stock**
salt and **pepper**

Herby couscous
200 g (7 oz) **couscous**
150 g (5 oz) cooked **beetroot**,
  peeled and diced
400 ml (14 fl oz) boiling **water**
grated rind and juice of
  1 **lemon**
2 tablespoons **olive oil**
small bunch of **parsley**, finely
  chopped
small bunch of **mint**, finely
  chopped

Preheat the slow cooker if necessary; see the manufacturer's instructions. Heat the oil in a frying pan, add the lamb and fry on both sides until browned. Lift out with two slotted spoons and transfer to the slow cooker pot. Fry the onion, stirring, for 5 minutes or until softened and just turning golden.

Stir in the garlic, then the flour. Add the mint jelly and wine and mix until smooth. Pour in the stock, season and bring to the boil, stirring. Pour the sauce over the lamb, cover with the lid and cook on high for 7–8 hours or until the lamb is almost falling off the bone.

When almost ready to serve, put the couscous and beetroot into a bowl, pour over the boiling water, then add the lemon rind and juice, oil and some seasoning. Cover with a plate and leave to soak for 5 minutes.

Add the herbs to the couscous and fluff up with a fork, then spoon on to plates. Lift the lamb on to a serving plate and carve into rough pieces, discarding the bone. Divide between the plates and serve the sauce separately in a jug to pour over as needed.

For coriander & honey-braised lamb, fry the onion and garlic as above. Add 1 tablespoon roughly crushed coriander seeds with the flour. Stir in 1 tablespoon set honey instead of the mint jelly and 150 ml (¼ pint) dry white wine instead of red. Add the lamb stock, 1 bay leaf and seasoning. Bring to the boil, then add to the browned lamb in the slow cooker pot. Cover and cook as above. Serve with rice and green beans.

chicken korma

Preparation time **20 minutes**
Cooking temperature **low**
Cooking time **6–8 hours**
Serves **4**

2 tablespoons **sunflower oil**
8 **chicken thighs**, about 1 kg
(2 lb) in total, skinned,
boned and cubed
2 **onions**, finely chopped, plus
extra to garnish
1–2 **green chillies** (to taste),
deseeded and finely
chopped
2.5 cm (1 inch) **fresh root
ginger**, peeled and finely
chopped
5 tablespoons **korma curry
paste**
250 ml (8 fl oz) **coconut
cream** or **milk**
300 ml (½ pint) **chicken stock**
2 tablespoons **ground
almonds**
small bunch of **coriander**
200 g (7 oz) **natural yogurt**
2 **tomatoes**, diced
salt and **pepper**
warm **chapatis**, to serve

Preheat the slow cooker if necessary; see the manufacturer's instructions. Heat the oil in a frying pan, add the chicken a few pieces at time until it is all in the pan, then fry, stirring, until golden. Remove from the pan with a slotted spoon and put in the slow cooker pot.

Add the onions, green chillies, ginger and curry paste to the pan and fry, stirring, for 2–3 minutes. Pour in the coconut cream or milk, stock and ground almonds. Tear half the coriander into pieces and add to the sauce with a little salt and pepper. Bring to the boil, stirring, then spoon over the chicken.

Cover with the lid and cook on low for 6–8 hours. Stir the korma then ladle into bowls, top with spoonfuls of yogurt, the tomatoes and extra raw onion and the remaining coriander torn into small pieces. Serve with warm chapatis.

For fish korma, omit the chicken and fry the onions, chillies, ginger and curry paste in the oil as above. Mix in the coconut cream or milk, 300 ml (½ pint) fish stock instead of chicken stock and the ground almonds, coriander and salt and pepper. Bring to the boil then pour into the slow cooker pot. Add 2 large cod loins, about 500 g (1 lb) in total, press beneath the sauce and cook on low for 2–2¼ hours or until the fish flakes when pressed with a knife.

steak & mushroom pudding

Preparation time **40 minutes**
Cooking temperature **high**
Cooking time **5–6 hours**
Serves **4**

25 g (1 oz) **butter**, plus extra
for greasing
1 tablespoon **sunflower oil**
2 large **onions**, roughly
chopped
2 teaspoons **caster sugar**
100 g (3½ oz) **cup
mushrooms**, sliced
1 tablespoon **plain** or **self-
raising flour**
150 ml (¼ pint) hot **beef
stock**
1 teaspoon **Dijon mustard**
1 tablespoon **Worcestershire
sauce**
700 g (1 lb 6 oz) **rump steak**,
thinly sliced and any fat
discarded
salt and **pepper**

Pastry
300 g (10 oz) **self-raising
flour**
½ teaspoon **salt**
150 g (5 oz) shredded **suet**
200 ml (7 fl oz) **water**

Preheat the slow cooker if necessary; see the
manufacturer's instructions. Heat the butter and oil in a
frying pan, add the onions and fry for 5 minutes or until
softened. Sprinkle the sugar over the onions and fry for
5 more minutes or until browned. Add the mushrooms
and fry for 2–3 minutes. Stir in the flour.

Mix together the stock, mustard, Worcestershire sauce
and salt and pepper in a jug.

Make the suet pastry. Put the flour, salt and suet in a
bowl and mix well. Gradually stir in enough water to make
a soft but not sticky dough. Knead the dough lightly, then
roll out on a floured surface to a circle 33 cm (13 inches)
across. Cut out a quarter segment and reserve.

Press the remaining dough into a 1.5 litre (2½ pint)
buttered pudding basin, butting the edges together.

Layer the fried onions, mushrooms and sliced steak in the
basin. Pour the stock over the top. Pat the reserved pastry
into a round the same size as the top of the basin. Fold
the top edges of the pastry in the basin over the filling,
brush with a little water and cover with the pastry lid.

Cover the pudding with a large domed circle of
buttered foil so that there is room for the pastry to rise.
Tie with string. Stand the basin in the slow cooker pot
on top of an upturned saucer. Pour boiling water into
the pot to come halfway up the sides of the basin.
Cover with the lid and cook on high for 5–6 hours.

Remove the basin from the slow cooker using a tea
towel and remove the string and foil. The pastry should
have risen and feel dry to the touch.

rancheros pie

Preparation time **25 minutes**
Cooking temperature **low**
Cooking time **7–8 hours**
Serves **4**

1 tablespoon **sunflower oil**
500 g (1 lb) **minced beef**
1 **onion**, chopped
2 **garlic cloves**, finely
  chopped
1 teaspoon **cumin seeds**,
  roughly crushed
¼–½ teaspoon **crushed dried
  red chillies**
¼ teaspoon **ground allspice**
2 stems of **oregano**, roughly
  chopped
3 tablespoons **sultanas**
400 g (13 oz) can **chopped
  tomatoes**
250 ml (8 fl oz) **beef stock**
salt and **pepper**

Topping
500 g (1 lb) **sweet potatoes**,
  thinly sliced
25 g (1 oz) **butter**
few **crushed dried red
  chillies**

Preheat the slow cooker if necessary; see the manufacturer's instructions. Heat the oil in a frying pan, add the beef and onion and fry, stirring and breaking up the mince with a wooden spoon, until browned.

Stir in the garlic, spices, oregano, sultanas, tomatoes and stock. Add a little salt and pepper and bring to the boil, stirring. Spoon into the slow cooker pot, cover with overlapping slices of sweet potato, dot with butter and sprinkle with dried chillies and a little salt and pepper.

Cover with the lid and cook on low for 7–8 hours until the potato topping is tender. Lift the pot out of the housing using oven gloves and brown under a hot grill, if liked.

For cowboy pie, fry the mince and onion as above, then omit the garlic, spices, oregano, sultanas and tomatoes but add 2 tablespoons Worcestershire sauce, 410 g (13½ oz) can baked beans, 1 bay leaf and 200 ml (7 fl oz) beef stock. Cook the mince base as above. Top with 750 g (1½ lb) potatoes, cooked and mashed with butter and salt and pepper. Sprinkle with 50 g (2 oz) grated Cheddar cheese and brown under the grill.

caribbean chicken with rice & peas

Preparation time **20 minutes**
Cooking temperature **low** and
high
Cooking time **7−9 hours**
Serves **4**

8 **chicken thighs**, about 1 kg
(2 lb) in total
3 tablespoons **jerk marinade**
(see below)
2 tablespoons **sunflower oil**
2 large **onions**, chopped
2 **garlic cloves**, finely
chopped
400 ml (14 fl oz) can **full-fat
coconut milk**
300 ml (½ pint) **chicken stock**
410 g (13½ oz) can **red
kidney beans**, drained
200 g (7 oz) easy-cook **long-
grain rice**
125 g (4 oz) frozen **peas**
salt and **pepper**

To garnish
lime wedges
sprigs of **coriander**

Preheat the slow cooker if necessary; see the manufacturer's instructions. Remove the skin from the chicken thighs, slash each thigh 2−3 times and rub with the jerk marinade.

Heat 1 tablespoon oil in a large frying pan, add the chicken and fry over a high heat until browned on both sides. Lift out with a slotted spoon and transfer to a plate. Add the remaining oil, the onions and garlic, reduce the heat and fry for 5 minutes or until softened and lightly browned. Pour in the coconut milk and stock, season with salt and pepper and bring to the boil.

Transfer half the mixture to the slow cooker pot, add half the chicken pieces, all the beans and then the remaining chicken, onions and coconut mixture. Cover, cook on low for 6−8 hours until the chicken is tender.

Stir in the rice, replace the lid and cook on high for 45 minutes. Add the frozen peas (no need to thaw) and cook for a further 15 minutes. Spoon on to plates and serve garnished with lime wedges and coriander sprigs.

For jerk marinade, halve 1−2 scotch bonnet chillies, depending on their size, discard the seeds and chop finely. Put in a clean screw-top jar with 1 tablespoon finely chopped thyme leaves, 1 teaspoon ground allspice, 1 teaspoon ground cinnamon, ½ teaspoon grated nutmeg, ½ teaspoon salt, ½ teaspoon ground black pepper, 3 teaspoons brown sugar, 2 tablespoons sunflower oil and 4 tablespoons cider vinegar. Add the lid and shake to mix. Use 3 tablespoons of the marinade and store the remainder in the refrigerator for up to 2 weeks.

beef adobo

Preparation time **25 minutes**
Cooking temperature **low**
Cooking time **8–10 hours**
Serves **4**

1 tablespoon **sunflower oil**
750 g (1 ½ lb) **braising beef**,
    cubed and any fat discarded
1 large **onion**, sliced
2 **garlic cloves**, finely
    chopped
2 tablespoons **plain flour**
450 ml (¾ pint) **beef stock**
4 tablespoons **soy sauce**
4 tablespoons **wine vinegar**
1 tablespoon **caster sugar**
2 **bay leaves**
juice of 1 **lime**
salt and **pepper**
long-grain rice, to serve

To garnish
1 **carrot**, cut into thin sticks
½ bunch of **spring onions**,
    cut into shreds
coriander leaves

Preheat the slow cooker if necessary; see the manufacturer's instructions. Heat the oil in a large frying pan and add the beef a few pieces at a time until all the meat has been added. Fry over a high heat, turning until evenly browned, lift out of the pan with a slotted spoon and transfer to a plate.

Add the onion to the pan and fry for 5 minutes or until it is just beginning to brown. Mix in the garlic and cook for 2 minutes. Stir in the flour, then gradually mix in the stock. Add the soy sauce, vinegar, sugar, bay leaves and salt and pepper and bring to the boil, stirring.

Transfer the beef to the slow cooker pot, pour over the onion and stock mixture, cover with the lid and cook on low for 8–10 hours.

Stir in lime juice to taste and garnish with carrot sticks, shredded spring onions and coriander leaves. Serve in shallow bowls lined with rice.

For hoisin beef, combine 3 tablespoons each soy sauce and rice or wine vinegar with 2 tablespoons hoisin sauce and 2.5 cm (1 inch) peeled and finely chopped fresh root ginger. Add this mixture to the beef stock with the sugar. Omit the bay leaves. Bring the mixture to the boil, then continue as above, adding the lime juice just before serving.

lamb tagine with figs & almonds

Preparation time **15 minutes**
Cooking temperature **low**
Cooking time **8–10 hours**
Serves **4**

1 tablespoon **olive oil**
750 g (1½ lb) **lamb fillet**, diced, or **ready-diced lamb**
1 **onion**, sliced
2 **garlic cloves**, finely chopped
2.5 cm (1 inch) **fresh root ginger**, peeled and finely chopped
2 tablespoons **plain flour**
600 ml (1 pint) **lamb stock**
1 teaspoon **ground cinnamon**
2 large pinches of **saffron threads**
75 g (3 oz) dried **figs**, stalks trimmed off and fruits diced
40 g (1½ oz) **toasted flaked almonds**
salt and **pepper**

Preheat the slow cooker if necessary; see the manufacturer's handbook. Heat the oil in a frying pan, add the lamb a few pieces at a time until all the pieces are added to the pan, then fry over a high heat, stirring until browned. Remove from the pan with a slotted spoon and transfer to the slow cooker pot.

Add the onion and fry, stirring, for 5 minutes or until softened and just beginning to turn golden. Stir in the garlic and ginger, then mix in the flour. Gradually stir in the stock. Add the spices, figs and a little salt and pepper and bring to the boil, stirring.

Spoon into the slow cooker pot, cover with the lid and cook on low for 8–10 hours or until the lamb is tender. Stir, then sprinkle with toasted flaked almonds. Serve with lemon and chickpea couscous (see below).

For lemon & chickpea couscous to accompany the tagine put 200 g (7 oz) couscous into a bowl, add the grated rind and juice of 1 lemon, 2 tablespoons olive oil, a drained 410 g (13½ oz) can chickpeas and some salt and pepper. Pour over 450 ml (¾ pint) boiling water, then cover the bowl with a plate and leave to stand for 5 minutes. Remove the plate, add 4 tablespoons chopped parsley or coriander and fluff up with a fork.

lemon chicken

Preparation time **20 minutes**
Cooking temperature **high**
Cooking time **3¼–4¼ hours**
Serves **4**

1 tablespoon **olive oil**
4 boneless, skinless **chicken breasts**, about 550 g (1 lb 2 oz) in total
1 **onion**, chopped
2 **garlic cloves**, finely chopped
2 tablespoons **plain flour**
450 ml (¾ pint) **chicken stock**
½ **lemon** (cut in half lengthways), cut into 4 wedges
2 **pak choi**, thickly sliced
125 g (4 oz) **sugar snap peas**, halved lengthways
4 tablespoons **crème fraîche**
2 tablespoons chopped **mint** and **parsley**, mixed
salt and **pepper**

To serve
couscous mixed with finely chopped **tomato, red onion** and **red pepper**

Preheat the slow cooker if necessary; see the manufacturer's instructions. Heat the oil in a large frying pan, add the chicken breasts and fry over a high heat until browned on both sides. Remove from the pan and transfer to a plate. Add the onion to the pan and fry, stirring, for 5 minutes or until lightly browned.

Stir in the garlic and flour, then mix in the stock and lemon wedges. Season with salt and pepper and bring to the boil.

Put the chicken breasts in the slow cooker pot, pour the hot stock mixture over them and press the chicken below the surface of the liquid. Cover with the lid and cook on high for 3–4 hours.

Add the pak choi and sugar snap peas and cook, still on high, for 15 minutes or until just tender. Lift out the chicken, slice the pieces and arrange them on plates. Stir the crème fraîche and herbs into the sauce, then spoon it and the vegetables over the chicken. Serve with couscous mixed with finely chopped tomato, red onion and red pepper.

For lemon chicken with harissa, add 4 teaspoons harissa paste to the frying pan with the chicken stock and wedges cut from ½ lemon. Continue as above. Omit the pak choi at the end, adding instead 125 g (4 oz) broccoli, the florets cut into small pieces and stems sliced and ½ courgette. Reduce the sugar snap peas to just 50 g (2 oz).

olive & lemon meatballs

Preparation time **30 minutes**
Cooking temperature **low**
Cooking time **6–8 hours**
Serves **4**

Meatballs
50 g (2 oz) pitted **black
olives**, chopped
grated rind of ½ **lemon**
500 g (1 lb) **extra-lean
minced beef**
1 **egg yolk**
1 tablespoon **olive oil**

Sauce
1 **onion**, chopped
2 **garlic cloves**, finely
chopped
400 g (13 oz) can **chopped
tomatoes**
1 teaspoon **caster sugar**
150 ml (¼ pint) **chicken stock**
salt and **pepper**
small **basil leaves**, to garnish
tagliatelle tossed with
chopped **basil** and **melted
butter**, to serve

Preheat the slow cooker if necessary; see the manufacturer's instructions. Make the meatballs. Put all the ingredients except for the oil in a bowl and mix with a wooden spoon. Wet your hands and shape the mixture into 20 balls.

Heat the oil in a large frying pan, add the meatballs and cook over a high heat, turning until browned on all sides. Lift them out of pan with a slotted spoon and transfer to a plate.

Make the sauce. Add the onion to the pan and fry, stirring, for 5 minutes or until lightly browned. Add the garlic, tomatoes, sugar, stock and salt and pepper and bring to the boil, stirring.

Transfer the meatballs to the slow cooker pot, pour over the hot sauce, cover and cook on low for 6–8 hours. Garnish with basil leaves and serve with tagliatelle tossed with chopped basil and melted butter.

For herb & garlic meatballs, replace the olives and lemon rind with 2 finely chopped garlic cloves and 3 tablespoons chopped basil leaves. Mix, shape and cook the meatballs with the sauce as above, adding a small handful of basil leaves to the sauce just before serving.

mustard chicken & bacon

Preparation time **15 minutes**
Cooking temperature **low**
Cooking time **8¼–10¼ hours**
Serves **4**

15 g (½ oz) **butter**
1 tablespoon **sunflower oil**
4 **chicken thigh** and
    4 **chicken drumstick** joints
4 rashers **smoked back**
    bacon, diced
400 g (13 oz) **leeks**, thinly
    sliced; white and green parts
    kept separate
2 tablespoons **plain flour**
600 ml (1 pint) **chicken stock**
3 teaspoons **wholegrain**
    mustard
salt and **pepper**
mashed **potato**, to serve

Preheat the slow cooker if necessary; see the manufacturer's instructions. Heat the butter and oil in a frying pan, add the chicken joints and fry over a high heat until browned on all sides. Transfer to the slow cooker pot with a slotted spoon.

Add the bacon and white sliced leeks to the frying pan and fry, stirring, for 5 minutes or until just beginning to turn golden. Stir in the flour, then gradually mix in the stock, mustard and a little salt and pepper. Bring to the boil. Pour into the slow cooker pot, cover with the lid and cook on low for 8–10 hours.

Add the green sliced leeks and stir into the sauce, then replace the lid and cook, still on low, for 15 minutes or until the green leeks are just softened. Spoon into shallow serving bowls and serve with mashed potato.

For mustard chicken & frankfurter casserole, fry the chicken as above, then drain and add to the slow cooker pot. Add 1 chopped onion to the pan, then mix in 4 chilled sliced frankfurters and fry for 5 minutes. Stir in the flour, then mix in the stock, mustard and seasoning as above. Add a 200 g (7 oz) can of drained sweetcorn, transfer to the slow cooker pot and cook on low for 8–10 hours.

beery barley beef

Preparation time **15 minutes**
Cooking temperature **low**
Cooking time **9–10 hours**
Serves **4**

1 tablespoon **sunflower oil**
625 g (1¼ lb) lean **stewing beef**, cubed
1 **onion**, chopped
1 tablespoon **plain flour**
250 g (8 oz) **carrots**, diced
250 g (8 oz) **parsnips** or **potatoes**, diced
300 ml (½ pint) **light ale**
750 ml (1¼ pint) **beef stock**
small bunch of **mixed herbs** or dried **bouquet garni**
100 g (3½ oz) **pearl barley**
salt and **pepper**

Preheat the slow cooker if necessary; see the manufacturer's instructions. Heat the oil in a frying pan, add the beef a few pieces at a time until it is all in the pan, then fry over a high heat, stirring, until browned. Remove the beef with a slotted spoon and transfer to the slow cooker pot.

Add the onion to the frying pan and fry, stirring, for 5 minutes or until lightly browned. Mix in the flour, then add the root vegetables and beer and bring to the boil, stirring. Pour into the slow cooker pot.

Add the stock to the frying pan with the herbs and a little salt and pepper, bring to the boil, then pour into the slow cooker pot. Add the pearl barley, cover with the lid and cook on low for 9–10 hours until the beef is tender. Serve with herb croutons (see below), if liked.

For herb croutons to accompany the beef beat 2 tablespoons chopped parsley, 2 tablespoons chopped chives and 1 tablespoon chopped tarragon and a little black pepper into 75 g (3 oz) soft butter. Thickly slice ½ French stick, toast lightly on both sides, then spread with the herb butter.

pot-roast pheasant with chestnuts

Preparation time **15 minutes**
Cooking temperature **high**
Cooking time **3–4 hours**
Serves **2–3**

1 **pheasant**, about 750 g
  (1½ lb)
25 g (1 oz) **butter**
1 tablespoon **olive oil**
200 g (7 oz) **shallots**, halved
50 g (2 oz) **smoked streaky**
  bacon, diced, or ready-diced
  pancetta
2 **celery sticks**, thickly sliced
1 tablespoon **plain flour**
300 ml (½ pint) **chicken stock**
4 tablespoons **dry sherry**
100 g (3½ oz) vacuum-packed
  prepared **chestnuts**
2–3 sprigs of **thyme**
salt and **pepper**
potatoes dauphinois,
  to serve

Preheat the slow cooker if necessary; see the manufacturer's instructions. Rinse the pheasant inside and out with plenty of cold running water, then pat fry with kitchen towel.

Heat the butter and oil in a frying pan, add the pheasant, breast side down, the shallots, bacon or pancetta and celery and fry until golden brown, turning the pheasant and stirring the other ingredients. Transfer the pheasant to the slow cooker pot, placing it breast side down.

Stir the flour into the onion mix. Gradually add the stock and sherry, then add the chestnuts, thyme and a little salt and pepper. Bring to the boil, stirring, then spoon over the pheasant. Cover with the lid and cook on high for 3–4 hours until tender. Test with a knife through the thickest part of the pheasant leg and breast to make sure that the juices run clear. Carve the pheasant breast into thick slices and cut the legs away from the body. Serve with potatoes dauphinois.

For pot-roast guinea fowl with prunes, fry a 1 kg (2 lb) guinea fowl instead of the pheasant as above. Transfer the fowl to the slow cooker, mix in 2 tablespoons plain flour, then add 450 ml (¾ pint) chicken stock and the sherry. Omit the chestnuts, and add 75 g (3 oz) halved, stoned prunes instead. Continue as above, but cook for 5–6 hours.

fish &
seafood

caribbean brown stew trout

Preparation time **20 minutes**
Cooking temperature **high**
Cooking time **1½–2 hours**
Serves **4**

4 small **trout**, gutted, heads
   and fins removed and well
   rinsed with cold water
1 teaspoon **ground allspice**
1 teaspoon **paprika**
1 teaspoon **ground coriander**
2 tablespoons **olive oil**
6 **spring onions**, thickly sliced
1 **red pepper**, cored,
   deseeded and thinly sliced
2 **tomatoes**, roughly chopped
½ **red hot bonnet** or other
   red chilli, deseeded and
   chopped
2 sprigs of **thyme**
300 ml (½ pint) **fish stock**
salt and **pepper**

Preheat the slow cooker if necessary; see the manufacturer's instructions. Slash the trout on each side 2–3 times with a sharp knife. Mix the spices and a little salt and pepper on a plate, then dip each side of the trout in the spice mix.

Heat the oil in a frying pan, add the trout and fry until browned on both sides but not cooked all the way through. Drain and arrange in the slow cooker pot with the fish resting on their lower edges and top to tailing them so that they fit snugly in a single layer.

Add the remaining ingredients to the frying pan with any spices left on the plate and bring to the boil, stirring. Pour over the trout, then cover with the lid and cook on high for 1½–2 hours or until the fish breaks into flakes when pressed in the centre with a knife.

Lift the fish carefully out of the slow cooker pot using a fish slice and transfer to shallow dishes. Spoon the sauce over and serve with warm bread to mop up the sauce, if liked.

For brown stew chicken, slash 8 chicken thigh joints instead of the trout and dip in the spice mix as above. Fry in the olive oil until browned, then drain and transfer to the slow cooker pot. Heat the vegetables as above with 450 ml (¾ pint) chicken stock, season, then cook with the chicken joints in the slow cooker on low for 8–10 hours. Thicken the sauce if liked with 4 teaspoons cornflour mixed with a little water, stir into the sauce and cook for 15 minutes more.

hot soused herrings

Preparation time **15 minutes**
Cooking temperature **high**
Cooking time **1½–2 hours**
Serves **4**

1 large **red onion**, thinly sliced
1 large **carrot**, cut into
    matchsticks
1 large **celery stick**, thinly
    sliced
6 small **herrings**, gutted,
    filleted and rinsed with cold
    water
2 stems of **tarragon**
1 **bay leaf**
150 ml (¼ pint) **cider vinegar**
25 g (1 oz) **caster sugar**
600 ml (1 pint) boiling **water**
½ teaspoon coloured
    peppercorns
salt
tarragon sprigs, to garnish

Preheat the slow cooker if necessary; see the manufacturer's instructions. Put half the onion, carrot and celery in the base of the slow cooker pot. Arrange the herring fillets on top then cover with the remaining vegetables.

Add the tarragon, bay leaf, vinegar and sugar, then pour over the boiling water. Add the peppercorns and a little salt. Cover with the lid and cook on high for 1½–2 hours.

Spoon the fish, vegetables and a little of the cooking liquid into shallow bowls, halving the fish fillets if liked. Garnish with tarragon sprigs. Serve with pickled beetroot, dill cucumbers and bread and butter, if liked.

For Swedish baked herrings, make as above, adding 2 sprigs of dill instead of the tarragon and increasing the amount of sugar to 50 g (2 oz). Leave to cool once cooked and serve with 8 tablespoons soured cream mixed with 1 teaspoon hot horseradish and accompanied with pickled cucumber salad.

salmon in hot miso broth

Preparation time **15 minutes**

Cooking temperature **low** and **high**

Cooking time **1 hour 40 minutes–2 hours 10 minutes**

Serves 6

4 **salmon steaks**, about 125 g (4 oz) each
1 **carrot**, thinly sliced
4 **spring onions**, thinly sliced
4 **cup mushrooms**, about 125 g (4 oz) in total, thinly sliced
1 large **red chilli**, halved, deseeded and finely chopped
2 cm (¾ inch) **fresh root ginger**, peeled and finely chopped
3 tablespoons **miso**
1 tablespoon dark **soy sauce**
2 tablespoons **mirin** (optional)
1.2 litres (2 pints) hot **fish stock**
75 g (3 oz) **mangetout**, thinly sliced
coriander leaves, to garnish

Preheat the slow cooker if necessary; see the manufacturer's instructions. Rinse the salmon in cold water, drain and place in the slow cooker pot. Arrange the carrot, spring onions, mushrooms, chilli and ginger on top of the fish.

Add the miso, soy sauce and mirin (if used) to the hot stock and stir until the miso has dissolved. Pour the stock mixture over the salmon and vegetables. Cover with the lid and cook on low for 1½–2 hours or until the fish is tender and the soup is piping hot.

Lift the fish out with a fish slice and transfer it to a plate. Flake it into chunky pieces, discarding the skin and any bones. Return the fish to the slow cooker pot and add the mangetout. Cook on high for 10 minutes or until the mangetout are just tender, then ladle the soup into bowls and garnish with coriander leaves.

For salmon in aromatic Thai broth, follow the recipe as above, adding 3 teaspoons Thai red curry paste, 3 small kaffir lime leaves and 2 teaspoons fish sauce instead of the miso and mirin.

mackerel with harissa potatoes

Preparation time **20 minutes**
Cooking temperature **low**
Cooking time **5–7 hours**
Serves **4**

500 g (1 lb) **new potatoes**,
 scrubbed and thickly sliced
1 tablespoon **olive oil**
1 **onion**, chopped
½ **red pepper**, cored,
 deseeded and diced
½ **yellow pepper**, cored,
 deseeded and diced
1 **garlic clove**, finely chopped
2 teaspoons **harissa**
 (Moroccan chilli paste)
200 g (7 oz) **tomatoes**,
 roughly chopped
1 tablespoon **tomato purée**
300 ml (½ pint) **fish stock**
4 small **mackerel**, each about
 300 g (10 oz), gutted and
 heads removed
salt and **pepper**

Preheat the slow cooker if necessary; see the manufacturer's instructions. Bring a saucepan of water to the boil, add the potatoes and cook for 4–5 minutes or until almost tender. Drain and reserve.

Heat the oil in a frying pan, add the onion and fry, stirring, for 5 minutes or until softened and just beginning to turn golden. Stir in the peppers and garlic and fry for 2–3 minutes. Mix in the harissa, tomatoes, tomato purée, stock and a little salt and pepper and bring to the boil.

Tip the potatoes into the base of the slow cooker pot. Rinse the fish well, drain and arrange in a single layer on top of the potatoes, then cover with the hot tomato mixture. Cover with the lid and cook on low for 5–7 hours or until the potatoes are tender and the fish flakes when pressed in the centre with a small knife.

Spoon into shallow bowls and serve with warmed pitta breads, if liked.

For harissa-spiced potatoes with feta, follow the recipe as above but omit the fish and instead sprinkle the top of the tomato mixture with 125 g (4 oz) drained and crumbled feta cheese and 50 g (2 oz) pitted black olives. Cook as above and sprinkle with torn parsley just before serving.

macaroni with smoked haddock

Preparation time **15 minutes**
Cooking temperature **low**
Cooking time **2¼–3¼ hours**
Serves **4**

200 g (7 oz) **macaroni**
1 tablespoon **olive oil**
1 **onion**, chopped
50 g (2 oz) **butter**
50 g (2 oz) **plain flour**
450 ml (¾ pint) **UHT milk**
450 ml (¾ pint) **fish stock**
175 g (6 oz) **Cheddar
cheese**, grated
¼ teaspoon grated **nutmeg**
500 g (1 lb) **smoked
haddock**, skinned and cut
into 2.5 cm (1 inch) cubes
200 g (7 oz) can **sweetcorn**,
drained
125 g (4 oz) **spinach**, rinsed,
drained and roughly torn
salt and **pepper**
grilled **cherry tomatoes** on
the vine, to serve

Preheat the slow cooker if necessary; see the manufacturer's instructions. Tip the macaroni into a bowl, cover with plenty of boiling water and leave to stand for 10 minutes while preparing the rest of the dish.

Heat the oil in a saucepan, add the onion and fry gently, stirring, for 5 minutes or until softened. Add the butter and, when melted, stir in the flour. Gradually mix in the milk and bring to the boil, stirring until smooth. Stir in the stock, 125 g (4 oz) of the cheese, nutmeg and salt and pepper and bring back to the boil, stirring.

Drain the macaroni and add to the slow cooker pot with the haddock and sweetcorn. Pour over the sauce and gently stir together. Cover with the lid and cook on low for 2–3 hours.

Stir the spinach into the macaroni, replace the lid and cook on low for 15 minutes. Lift the pot out of the housing using oven gloves and stir once more. Sprinkle the remaining cheese over the macaroni, then brown under a hot grill until the top is golden. Serve with grilled cherry tomatoes on the vine.

For Stilton macaroni with bacon, soak the macaroni as above. Make up the cheese sauce with the milk, adding vegetable stock in place of fish stock and replacing the Cheddar cheese with Stilton cheese. Omit the fish and cook as above with the sweetcorn. Stir in the spinach and 6 rashers grilled smoked back bacon, diced. Cook for 15 minutes, then finish with a little extra Stilton and brown under the grill.

tuna arrabiata

Preparation time **20 minutes**
Cooking temperature **low**
Cooking time **4–5 hours**
Serves **4**

1 tablespoon **olive oil**
1 **onion**, chopped
2 **garlic cloves**, finely
   chopped
1 **red pepper**, cored,
   deseeded and diced
1 teaspoon **smoked paprika**
   (pimenton)
¼–½ teaspoon **crushed**
   dried red chillies
400 g (13 oz) can **chopped**
   tomatoes
150 ml (¼ pint) **vegetable** or
   fish stock
200 g (7 oz) can **tuna** in
   water, drained
375 g (12 oz) **spaghetti**
salt and **pepper**

To serve
freshly grated **Parmesan**
   cheese
basil leaves

Preheat the slow cooker if necessary; see the manufacturer's instructions. Heat the oil in a frying pan, add the onion and fry, stirring, for 5 minutes or until just beginning to turn golden around the edges.

Stir in the garlic, red pepper, paprika and dried chillies and cook for 2 minutes. Mix in the tomatoes, stock and a little salt and pepper. Bring to the boil, then tip into the slow cooker pot. Break the tuna into large pieces and stir into the tomato mixture. Cover with the lid and cook on low for 4–5 hours.

When almost ready to serve, bring a large saucepan of water to the boil, add the spaghetti and cook for about 8 minutes or until tender. Drain and stir into the tomato sauce. Spoon into shallow bowls and sprinkle with grated Parmesan and basil leaves to taste.

For double tomato arrabiata, omit the tuna from the tomato sauce. Instead, mix in 75 g (3 oz) sliced sun-dried tomatoes and 100 g (3½ oz) sliced button mushrooms. Cook and serve as above.

chermoula poached salmon

Preparation time **15 minutes**
Cooking temperature **low**
Cooking time **1¾–2¼ hours**
Serves **4**

6 **spring onions**
25 g (1 oz) **parsley**
25 g (1 oz) **coriander**
grated rind and juice of
    1 **lemon**
4 tablespoons **olive oil**
½ teaspoon **cumin seeds**,
    roughly crushed
500 g (1 lb) thick end **salmon**
    fillet no longer than 18 cm
    (7 inches), skinned
250 ml (8 fl oz) **fish stock**
6 tablespoons **mayonnaise**
125 g (4 oz) mixed **salad**
    leaves
salt and **pepper**

Preheat the slow cooker if necessary; see the manufacturer's instructions. Finely chop the spring onions and herbs with a large knife or in a food processor if you have one. Mix with the lemon rind and juice, the oil, cumin seeds and a little salt and pepper.

Rinse the salmon with cold water, drain well and put on a long piece of kitchen foil, the width of the salmon. Press half the herb mixture over both sides of the salmon then use the foil to lower the fish into the slow cooker pot.

Bring the stock to the boil in a small saucepan, pour over the salmon and tuck the ends of the foil down if needed. Cover with the lid and cook on low for 1¾–2¼ hours or until the fish flakes into opaque pieces when pressed in the centre with a knife.

Lift the salmon out of the slow cooker pot using the foil and transfer to a serving plate. Mix the remaining uncooked herb mixture with the mayonnaise. Arrange the salad leaves on 4 plates. Cut the salmon into 4 pieces and place on the salad. Serve with spoonfuls of the herb mayonnaise.

For classic poached salmon, omit the chermoula herb mixture. Rinse the salmon as above, then lower into the slow cooker pot on a piece of foil. Add ½ sliced lemon, ½ sliced onion, 2 sprigs of tarragon and a little salt and pepper. Bring 200 ml (7 fl oz) fish stock and 4 tablespoons white wine to the boil in a small saucepan, pour over the fish and cook as above. Drain and serve hot or cold with salad and spoonfuls of plain mayonnaise.

squid in puttanesca sauce

Preparation time **25 minutes**
Cooking temperature **low**
Cooking time **3½–4½ hours**
Serves **4**

500 g (1 lb) prepared **squid tubes**
1 tablespoon **olive oil**
1 **onion**, chopped
2 **garlic cloves**, finely chopped
400 g (13 oz) can **chopped tomatoes**
150 ml (¼ pint) **fish stock**
4 teaspoons **capers**, drained
50 g (2 oz) pitted **black olives**
2–3 sprigs of **thyme**, plus extra to garnish (optional)
1 teaspoon **fennel seeds**, roughly crushed
1 teaspoon **caster sugar**
salt and **pepper**
linguine, to serve

Preheat the slow cooker if necessary; see the manufacturer's instructions. Take the tentacles out of the squid tubes and rinse inside the tubes with cold water. Put them in a sieve and rinse the outside of the tubes and the tentacles. Drain well, put the tentacles in a small bowl, cover and return to the refrigerator. Thickly slice the squid tubes.

Heat the oil in a large frying pan, add the onion and fry, stirring, for 5 minutes or until golden. Add the garlic and cook for 2 minutes. Stir in the tomatoes, stock, capers, olives, thyme, fennel seeds, sugar and salt and pepper and bring to the boil.

Pour the sauce into the slow cooker pot, add the sliced squid and press the pieces below the surface of the sauce. Cover and cook on low for 3–4 hours.

Stir the squid mixture and add the tentacles, pressing them below the surface of the sauce. Cook on low for 30 minutes. Serve tossed with linguine and garnished with extra thyme leaves, if liked.

For squid in red wine & tomato sauce, replace the stock, capers, olives and fennel seeds with 150 ml (¼ pint) red wine. Cook as above, then garnish with chopped parsley and serve with warm crusty bread.

smoked mackerel kedgeree

Preparation time **15 minutes**
Cooking temperature **low**
Cooking time **3¼–4¼ hours**
Serves **4**

1 tablespoon **sunflower oil**
1 **onion**, chopped
1 teaspoon **turmeric**
2 tablespoons **mango chutney**
750–900 ml (1¼–1½ pints) **vegetable stock**
1 **bay leaf**
175 g (6 oz) easy-cook **brown rice**
250 g (8 oz) or **3 smoked mackerel fillets**, skinned
100 g (3½ oz) frozen **peas**
25 g (1 oz) **watercress** or **rocket** leaves
4 **hard-boiled eggs**, cut into wedges
salt and **pepper**

Preheat the slow cooker if necessary; see the manufacturer's instructions. Heat the oil in a frying pan, add the onion and fry, stirring, for 5 minutes or until softened and just beginning to turn golden.

Stir in the turmeric, chutney, stock, bay leaf and a little salt and pepper and bring to the boil. Pour into the slow cooker pot and add the rice. Add the smoked mackerel to the pot in a single layer. Cover with the lid and cook on low for 3–4 hours or until the rice is tender and has absorbed almost all the stock.

Stir in the peas, breaking up the fish into chunky pieces. Add extra hot stock if needed. Cook for 15 minutes more. Stir in the watercress or rocket, spoon on to plates and garnish with wedges of egg.

For smoked haddock kedgeree with cardamom, make up the recipe as above but omit the mango chutney and instead add 4 crushed cardamom pods with their black seeds. Replace the smoked mackerel with 400 g (13 oz) skinned smoked haddock fillet, cut into 2 pieces. Continue as above, adding the peas and egg wedges at the end but omitting the rocket or watercress. Drizzle with 4 tablespoons double cream.

poached salmon with beurre blanc

Preparation time **25 minutes**
Cooking temperature **low**
Cooking time **1¾–2¼ hours**
Serves **4**

100 g (3½ oz) **butter**
1 large **onion**, thinly sliced
1 **lemon**, sliced
500 g (1 lb) piece of thick end
  salmon fillet, no longer than
  18 cm (7 inches)
1 **bay leaf**
200 ml (7 fl oz) dry **white
  wine**
150 ml (¼ pint) **fish stock**
3 tablespoons finely chopped
  chives, plus extra to garnish
salt and **pepper**
lemon slices, to garnish

Preheat the slow cooker if necessary; see the manufacturer's instructions. Brush inside the slow cooker pot with a little of the butter. Fold a large piece of kitchen foil into 3, then place it at the bottom of the pot with the ends sticking up to use as a strap. Arrange the onion slices and half of the lemon slices over the foil. Place the salmon, flesh side up, on top. Season with salt and pepper, then add the bay leaf and remaining lemon slices.

Pour the wine and stock into a saucepan, bring to the boil, then pour over the salmon. Fold the foil down if necessary to fit the cooker lid, then cook on low for 1¾–2¼ hours until the fish is opaque and flakes easily when pressed in the centre with a knife.

Lift the salmon carefully out of the pot using the foil strap, draining off as much liquid as possible. Transfer to a serving plate, discard the bay leaf, lemon and onion slices, and keep warm. Strain the cooking liquid into a saucepan and boil rapidly for 4–5 minutes or until reduced to about 4 tablespoons.

Reduce the heat and gradually whisk in small pieces of the remaining butter, little by little, until the sauce thickens and becomes creamy. (Don't be tempted to hurry making the sauce either by adding the butter in one go or by increasing the heat to the sauce, or you may find that it separates.) Stir in the chopped chives and adjust the seasoning if needed.

Cut the salmon into 4 portions, discard the skin and transfer to individual plates. Spoon a little of the sauce around the fish. Garnish with lemon slices and chives.

vegetables

herby stuffed peppers

Preparation time **20 minutes**
Cooking temperature **low**
Cooking time **4–5 hours**
Serves **4**

4 different coloured **peppers**
100 g (3½ oz) easy-cook
  brown rice
410 g (13½ oz) can
  chickpeas, drained
small bunch of **parsley**,
  roughly chopped
small bunch of **mint**, roughly
  chopped
1 **onion**, finely chopped
2 **garlic cloves**, finely
  chopped
½ teaspoon **smoked paprika**
1 teaspoon **ground allspice**
600 ml (1 pint) hot **vegetable
  stock**
salt and **pepper**

Preheat the slow cooker if necessary; see the manufacturer's instructions. Cut the top off each pepper, then remove the core and seeds.

Mix together the rice, chickpeas, herbs, onion, garlic, paprika and allspice with plenty of seasoning. Spoon the mixture into the insides of the peppers, then put the peppers into the slow cooker pot.

Pour the hot stock around the peppers, cover with the lid and cook on low for 4–5 hours or until the rice and peppers are tender. Spoon into dishes and serve with salad and spoonfuls of Greek yogurt flavoured with extra chopped herbs, if liked.

For feta-stuffed peppers, make the recipe as above, but use 100 g (3½ oz) crumbled feta cheese, 40 g (1½ oz) sultanas, a small bunch of chopped basil and ¼ teaspoon ground allspice instead of the chopped parsley, mint, paprika and allspice.

mushroom & walnut cobbler

Preparation time **30 minutes**
Cooking temperature **low** and **high**
Cooking time **6¾–8¾ hours**
Serves **4**

2 tablespoons **olive oil**
1 **onion**, chopped
2 **garlic cloves**, chopped
250 g (8 oz) **flat mushrooms**, peeled and quartered
250 g (8 oz) **cup chestnut mushrooms**, quartered
1 tablespoon **plain flour**
200 ml (7 fl oz) **red wine**
400 g (13 oz) can **chopped tomatoes**
150 ml (¼ pint) **vegetable stock**
1 tablespoon **redcurrant jelly**
2–3 stems of **thyme**
salt and **pepper**

Walnut topping
200 g (7 oz) **self-raising flour**
50 g (2 oz) **butter**, diced
50 g (2 oz) **walnut** pieces, chopped
75 g (3 oz) **Cheddar cheese**, grated
1 **egg**, beaten
4–5 tablespoons **milk**

Preheat the slow cooker if necessary; see the manufacturer's instructions. Heat the oil in a frying pan, add the onion, garlic and mushrooms and fry, stirring, for 5 minutes or until just turning golden.

Stir in the flour, then mix in the wine, tomatoes and stock. Add the redcurrant jelly, thyme and salt and pepper and bring to the boil. Pour into the slow cooker pot, cover with the lid and cook on low for 6–8 hours.

When almost ready to serve, make the topping. Put the flour and butter in a bowl, rub in the butter with your fingertips until fine breadcrumbs form. Stir in the walnuts, cheese and salt and pepper. Add half the egg, then mix in enough milk to make a soft dough.

Knead lightly, then roll out the dough on a lightly floured surface until 2 cm (¾ inch) thick. Stamp out 8 rounds with a 6 cm (2½ inch) plain biscuit cutter, re-rolling trimmings as needed. Stir the mushroom casserole, then arrange the scones, slightly overlapping, around the edge of the dish. Cover and cook on high for 45 minutes or until well risen. Lift the pot out of the housing using oven gloves, brush the tops of the scones with the remaining egg and brown under a grill, if liked.

For cheat's mushroom pie, make up the mushroom casserole as above, but omit the stock and scone topping. Unroll one pastry sheet from a 425 g (14 oz) pack of 2 and trim the edges to make an oval shape. Transfer to an oiled baking sheet, brush with beaten egg and bake in a preheated oven at 200°C (400°F), Gas Mark 6, for 15–20 minutes or until golden. Cut into wedge shapes and serve on top of the casserole.

green bean risotto with pesto

Preparation time **20 minutes**
Cooking temperature **low**
Cooking time **2 hours**
  5 minutes–2½ hours
Serves **4**

25 g (1 oz) **butter**
1 tablespoon **olive oil**
1 **onion**, chopped
2 **garlic cloves**, chopped
250 g (8 oz) **risotto rice**
1.2 litres (2¼ pints) hot
  vegetable stock
2 teaspoons **pesto**
125 g (4 oz) extra fine frozen
  green beans
125 g (4 oz) frozen **peas**
salt and **pepper**

To garnish
Parmesan shavings
basil leaves

Preheat the slow cooker if necessary; see the manufacturer's instructions. Heat the butter and oil in a saucepan, add the onion and fry, stirring, for 5 minutes or until softened and just beginning to brown.

Stir in the garlic and rice and cook for 1 minute. Add all but 150 ml (¼ pint) of the stock, season with salt and pepper, then bring to the boil. Transfer to the slow cooker pot, cover with the lid and cook on low for 1¾–2 hours.

Stir in the pesto and the remaining stock if more liquid is needed. Place the frozen vegetables on top of the rice, replace the lid and cook for another 20–30 minutes or until the vegetables are hot. Serve, garnished with Parmesan shavings and basil leaves.

For green bean risotto with sage & pancetta,
add 75 g (3 oz) diced pancetta or smoked streaky bacon when frying the chopped onion. Add 2 stems of sage to the mixture when adding the stock instead of the pesto. Replace the basil leaves with some tiny sage leaves.

warm beetroot & bean salad

Preparation time **25 minutes**
Cooking temperature **low**
Cooking time **3½—4½ hours**
Serves **4—5**

1 tablespoon **olive oil**
1 large **onion**, chopped
500 g (1 lb) raw **beetroot**,
    peeled and finely diced
2 × 410 g (13½ oz) cans
    borlotti beans, rinsed and
    drained
450 ml (¾ pint) **vegetable
    stock**
salt and **pepper**

To serve
¼ **cucumber**, finely diced
200 g (7 oz) **natural yogurt**
1 cos or iceberg **lettuce**
4 red- or white-stemmed
    spring onions, thinly sliced
4 tablespoons chopped fresh
    coriander or **mint** leaves

Preheat the slow cooker if necessary; see the manufacturer's instructions. Heat the oil in a frying pan, add the onion and fry, stirring, for 5 minutes or until pale golden. Add the beetroot to the pan with the drained beans, stock and plenty of salt and pepper. Bring to the boil, stirring.

Transfer the beetroot mixture to the slow cooker pot. Cover with the lid and cook on low for 3½—4½ hours or until the beetroot is tender. Stir well and lift the pot out of the cooker.

Stir the cucumber into the yogurt and season with salt and pepper. Arrange the lettuce leaves on 4—5 individual plates. Top with the warm beetroot salad, then add spoonfuls of the cucumber yogurt. Scatter the spring onions and coriander or mint over the top and serve at once.

For warm beetroot salad with feta & tomatoes, prepare the salad as above. Mix 125 g (4 oz) crumbled feta cheese with 2 diced tomatoes. Core, deseed and dice ½ red or orange pepper and combine with the cheese and tomatoes. Add 4 tablespoons chopped mint and 2 tablespoons olive oil. Spoon over the warm salad and top with 50 g (2 oz) rocket leaves.

sweet potato & egg curry

Preparation time **15 minutes**
Cooking temperature **low**
Cooking time **6–8 hours**
Serves **4**

1 tablespoon **sunflower oil**
1 **onion**, chopped
1 teaspoon **cumin seeds**,
  roughly crushed
1 teaspoon **ground coriander**
1 teaspoon **turmeric**
1 teaspoon **garam masala**
½ teaspoon **crushed dried
  red chillies**
300 g (10 oz) **sweet
  potatoes**, diced
2 **garlic cloves**, finely
  chopped
400 g (13 oz) can **chopped
  tomatoes**
410 g (13½ oz) can **lentils**,
  drained
300 ml (½ pint) **vegetable
  stock**
1 teaspoon **caster sugar**
6 **eggs**
150 g (5 oz) frozen **peas**
150 ml (¼ pint) **double
  cream**
small bunch of **coriander**, torn
  into pieces
salt and **pepper**

Preheat the slow cooker if necessary; see the manufacturer's instructions. Heat the oil in a frying pan, add the onion and fry, stirring, for 5 minutes or until softened and just beginning to turn golden.

Stir in the spices, dried chillies, sweet potatoes and garlic and fry for 2 minutes. Add the tomatoes, lentils, stock and sugar and season with a little salt and pepper. Bring to the boil, stirring. Spoon into the slow cooker pot, cover with the lid and cook on low for 6–8 hours.

When almost ready to serve, put the eggs in a small saucepan, cover with cold water and bring to the boil, then simmer for 8 minutes. Drain, crack the shells and cool under cold running water. Peel and halve, then add to the slow cooker pot with the peas, cream and half the coriander. Cover and cook on low for 15 minutes.

Spoon into bowls, garnish with the remaining coriander and serve with rice or warmed naan bread, if liked.

For sweet potato & paneer curry, make up the curry as above, adding 400 g (13 oz) diced paneer (Indian cheese) instead of the boiled eggs, reducing the peas to 100 g (3½ oz) and adding 100 g (3½ oz) baby corn cobs, halved if large.

mushroom & chestnut pudding

Preparation time **45 minutes**
Cooking temperature **high**
Cooking time **5–6 hours**
Serves **4**

Sauce
15 g (½ oz) **butter**
1 tablespoon **sunflower oil**
1 **onion**, thinly sliced
1 tablespoon **plain flour**
300 ml (½ pint) **vegetable
 stock**
5 tablespoons **ruby Port**
1 teaspoon **Dijon mustard**
1 teaspoon **tomato purée**
salt and **pepper**

Pastry
300 g (10 oz) **self-raising
 flour**
½ teaspoon **salt**
150 g (5 oz) **vegetable suet**
2 tablespoons finely chopped
 rosemary leaves
about 200 ml (7 fl oz) **water**

Filling
1 large **flat mushroom**, sliced
125 g (4 oz) **chestnut cup
 mushrooms**, sliced
200 g (7 oz) vacuum-packed
 whole peeled **chestnuts**

Preheat the slow cooker if necessary; see the manufacturer's instructions. Make the sauce. Heat the butter and oil in a large frying pan, add the onion and fry for 5 minutes. Stir in the flour, then mix in the stock, port, mustard and tomato purée. Season with salt and pepper, bring to the boil, stirring, then take off the heat.

Make the pastry. Mix together the flour, salt, suet and rosemary. Gradually add enough cold water to mix to a soft but not sticky dough. Knead lightly, then roll out on a floured surface to a circle 33 cm (13 inches) across. Cut a quarter segment from the circle of pastry and reserve.

Lift the remaining pastry into an oiled 1.25 litre (2¼ pint) pudding basin and bring the cut edges together, overlapping them slightly so that the basin is completely lined with pastry, then press them together to seal. Layer the sauce, mushrooms and chestnuts into the basin, finishing with the sauce.

Pat the reserved pastry into a circle the same size as the top of the basin. Dampen the edges of the pastry in the basin with a little water and press the lid in place. Cover with oiled foil and dome the foil slightly. Tie in place with string, then put into the slow cooker pot.

Pour boiling water into the slow cooker pot so that it comes halfway up the sides of the basin. Cover and cook on high for 5–6 hours.

For rosemary pudding with shallots & Madeira, make the sauce as above with 1 finely chopped onion and add 5 tablespoons Madeira instead of the Port. Replace the peeled chestnuts with shallots. Continue as above.

spinach & courgette tian

Preparation time **20 minutes**
Cooking temperature **high**
Cooking time **1½–2 hours**
Serves **4**

50 g (2 oz) **long-grain rice**
butter for greasing
1 **tomato**, sliced
1 tablespoon **olive oil**
½ **onion**, chopped
1 **garlic clove**, finely chopped
1 **courgette**, about 175 g
  (6 oz), coarsely grated
125 g (4 oz) **spinach**, thickly
  shredded
3 **eggs**
6 tablespoons **milk**
pinch of grated **nutmeg**
4 tablespoons chopped **mint**
salt and **pepper**

Preheat the slow cooker if necessary; see the manufacturer's instructions. Bring a small saucepan of water to the boil, add the rice, bring back to the boil, then simmer for 8–10 minutes or until tender. Meanwhile, butter the inside of a soufflé dish that is 14 cm (5½ inches) across the base and 9 cm (3½ inches) high. Base-line with nonstick baking paper, and arrange tomato slices, overlapping, on top.

Heat the oil in a frying pan, add the onion and fry, stirring, for 5 minutes or until softened and just beginning to turn golden. Stir in the garlic, then add the courgette and spinach and cook for 2 minutes or until the spinach is just wilted.

Beat together the eggs, milk, nutmeg and a little salt and pepper. Drain the rice and stir into the spinach mixture with the egg mixture and mint. Mix well, then spoon into the dish. Cover loosely with buttered foil and lower into the slow cooker pot with foil straps (see page 15) or tie string around the top edge.

Pour boiling water into the slow cooker pot to come halfway up the sides of the dish. Cover and cook on high for 1½–2 hours or until the tian is set in the middle. Lift out of the slow cooker, leave to stand for 5 minutes then remove the foil, loosen the edge and turn out on to a plate. Cut into wedges and serve warm with salad, if liked.

For cheesy spinach & pine nut tian, omit the courgette and instead stir in 50 g (2 oz) freshly grated Parmesan cheese, a small bunch of chopped basil and 4 tablespoons toasted pine nuts.

dum aloo

Preparation time **15 minutes**
Cooking temperature **high**
Cooking time **6¼–7¼ hours**
Serves **4**

2 tablespoons **sunflower oil**
1 large **onion**, sliced
1 teaspoon **cumin seeds**,
  crushed
4 **cardamom pods**, crushed
1 teaspoon **black onion
  seeds** (optional)
1 teaspoon **ground turmeric**
½ teaspoon **ground
  cinnamon**
2.5 cm (1 inch) **fresh root
  ginger**, peeled and finely
  chopped
400 g (13 oz) can **chopped
  tomatoes**
300 ml (½ pint) **vegetable
  stock**
1 teaspoon **caster sugar**
750 g (1½ lb) baby **new
  potatoes**
100 g (3½ oz) baby **leaf
  spinach**
salt and **pepper**
coriander leaves, to garnish
warm **naan bread**, to serve

Preheat the slow cooker if necessary; see the manufacturer's instructions. Heat the oil in a large frying pan, add the onion and fry, stirring, for 5 minutes or until lightly browned.

Mix in the cumin seeds, cardamom pods and seeds, onion seeds (if used), ground spices and ginger. Cook for 1 minute, then mix in the tomatoes, stock, sugar and season with salt and pepper. Bring to the boil, stirring.

Cut the potatoes into thick slices or halves (if they are small) so that all the pieces are of a similar size. Transfer to the slow cooker pot and pour the sauce over the top. Cover and cook on high for 6–7 hours or until the potatoes are tender.

Add the spinach and cook, still on high, for 15 minutes more until it is just wilted. Stir the curry and serve sprinkled with torn coriander leaves and accompanied with warm naan bread and a lentil dhal and plain rice, if liked.

For dum aloo with saffron & chickpeas, add 2 large pinches of saffron threads instead of the turmeric and mix into the pan when you add the tomatoes. Reduce the amount of potatoes to 500 g (1 lb). Drain a 410 g (13½ oz) can chickpeas and stir into the mixture. Pour over the hot sauce and cook as above.

moroccan seven-vegetable stew

Preparation time **25 minutes**
Cooking temperature **low** and **high**
Cooking time **6¼ hours– 8 hours 20 minutes**
Serves **4**

2 tablespoons **olive oil**
1 large **onion**, chopped
2 **carrots**, diced
300 g (10 oz) **swede**, diced
1 **red pepper**, cored, deseeded and chopped
3 **garlic cloves**, finely chopped
200 g (7 oz) frozen **broad beans**
400 g (13 oz) can **chopped tomatoes**
3 teaspoons **harissa** (Moroccan chilli paste)
1 teaspoon **ground turmeric**
2 cm (¾ inch) **fresh root ginger**, peeled and finely chopped
250 ml (8 fl oz) **vegetable stock**
125 g (4 oz) **okra**, thickly sliced
salt and **pepper**
mint leaves, torn, to garnish

Preheat the slow cooker if necessary; see the manufacturer's instructions. Heat the oil in a large frying pan, add the onion and fry, stirring, for 5 minutes or until lightly browned.

Add the carrots and swede to pan with the red pepper, garlic, beans and tomatoes. Mix in the harissa, turmeric and ginger, then pour on the stock and season with salt and pepper. Bring to the boil, stirring.

Spoon the mixture into the slow cooker pot and press the vegetables beneath the surface of the stock. Cover and cook on low for 6–8 hours or until the root vegetables are tender.

Stir in the okra, cover and cook on high for 15–20 minutes or until the okra are tender but still bright green. Garnish with mint leaves and serve with couscous soaked in boiling water and flavoured with olive oil, lemon juice and sultanas.

For Moroccan beef & vegetable stew, fry the onion with 300 g (10 oz) minced beef, then add just 1 chopped carrot and 150 g (5 oz) diced swede, the red pepper, garlic, 125 g (4 oz) frozen broad beans and the chopped tomatoes. Add the remaining ingredients and cook in the slow cooker for 8–10 hours. Add the okra and finish as above.

ratatouille with ricotta dumplings

Preparation time **25 minutes**
Cooking temperature **high**
Cooking time **3¼–4 hours
20 minutes**
Serves **4**

3 tablespoons **olive oil**
1 **onion**, chopped
1 **aubergine**, sliced
2 **courgettes**, about 375 g
(12 oz) in total, sliced
1 **red pepper**, cored,
deseeded and cubed
1 **yellow pepper**, cored,
deseeded and cubed
2 **garlic cloves**, finely
chopped
1 tablespoon **plain flour**
400 g (13 oz) can **chopped
tomatoes**
300 ml (½ pint) **vegetable
stock**
2–3 stems of **rosemary**
salt and **pepper**

Dumplings
100 g (3½ oz) **plain flour**
75 g (3 oz) **ricotta cheese**
grated rind of ½ **lemon**
1 **egg**, beaten

Preheat the slow cooker if necessary; see the manufacturer's instructions. Heat the oil in a frying pan, add the onion and aubergine and fry, stirring, for 5 minutes or until softened and just beginning to turn golden.

Stir in the courgettes, peppers and garlic and fry for 3–4 minutes. Mix in the flour, then the tomatoes, stock, rosemary and a little salt and pepper. Bring to the boil, then spoon into the slow cooker pot. Cover and cook on high for 3–4 hours until the vegetables are tender.

When almost ready to serve, make the dumplings. Put the flour, ricotta, lemon rind and a little salt and pepper into a bowl. Add the egg and mix to a soft but not sticky dough. Cut into 12 pieces and roll each piece into a ball with floured hands.

Stir the ratatouille and arrange the dumplings on the top. Replace the lid and cook for 15–20 minutes or until light and firm to the touch. Spoon into bowls and eat with a spoon and fork.

For chakchouka, make up the ratatouille as above and, when cooked, make 4 depressions in the vegetables with a spoon. Break an egg into each depression, then cover the slow cooker pot and cook on high for 10–15 minutes or until the eggs are just set. Spoon into shallow dishes to serve.

mixed mushroom & lentil braise

Preparation time **25 minutes**
Cooking temperature **low**
Cooking time **6–8 hours**
Serves **4**

2 tablespoons **olive oil**, plus
    extra to serve
1 large **onion**, chopped
3 **garlic cloves**, chopped
400 g (13 oz) can **chopped
    tomatoes**
300 ml (½ pint) **vegetable
    stock**
150 ml (¼ pint) **red wine**
    (or extra stock)
1 tablespoon **tomato purée**
2 teaspoons **caster sugar**
125 g (4 oz) **Puy lentils**
375 g (12 oz) **cup
    mushrooms**, halved or
    quartered
125 g (4 oz) **shiitake
    mushrooms**, halved if large
4 large **field mushrooms**,
    about 250 g (8 oz) in total
salt and **pepper**

To serve
rocket leaves
Parmesan cheese shavings
fried rounds of **polenta**

Preheat the slow cooker if necessary; see the manufacturer's instructions. Heat the oil in a large frying pan, add the onion and fry, stirring, for 5 minutes or until lightly browned. Mix in the garlic, tomatoes, stock, wine (if used), tomato purée and sugar and season with salt and pepper. Add the Puy lentils and bring to the boil.

Put the mushrooms in the slow cooker pot and pour over the lentil mixture, then cover and cook on low for 6–8 hours, stirring once if possible.

Serve with rocket leaves tossed with Parmesan shavings and a drizzle of olive oil and fried rounds of polenta.

For mixed mushroom & lentil cheesy bake, make and cook the mushroom and lentil mixture as above. Mix together 3 eggs, 250 g (8 oz) natural yogurt, 75 g (3 oz) grated feta cheese and a pinch of grated nutmeg. Press the cooked mushroom mixture into an even layer, then spoon the yogurt mix on top. Arrange 2 sliced tomatoes on top and cook on high for 45 minutes–1¼ hours until the topping is set. Lift the pot out of the housing using oven gloves and brown under a hot grill, if liked.

pumpkin & parmesan gnocchi

Preparation time **20 minutes**
Cooking temperature **low**
Cooking time **6—8 hours**
Serves **4**

1 tablespoon **olive oil**
25 g (1 oz) **butter**
1 **onion**, thinly sliced
2 **garlic cloves**, finely
  chopped
2 tablespoons **plain flour**
150 ml (¼ pint) dry **white
  wine**
300 ml (½ pint) **vegetable
  stock**
2—3 stems of **sage**, plus extra
  to garnish (optional)
400 g (13 oz) **pumpkin** (or
  butternut squash),
  deseeded, peeled, diced and
  weighed after preparation
500 g (1 lb) chilled **gnocchi**
125 ml (4 fl oz) **double cream**
freshly grated **Parmesan
  cheese**
salt and **pepper**

Preheat the slow cooker if necessary; see the
manufacturer's instructions. Heat the oil and butter in a
frying pan, add the onion and fry, stirring, for 5 minutes
or until just beginning to turn golden.

Stir in the garlic, cook for 2 minutes, then stir in the
flour. Gradually mix in the wine and stock and heat,
stirring until smooth. Add the sage and season well.

Add the pumpkin to the slow cooker pot, pour over the
hot sauce, then press the pumpkin beneath the surface
of the liquid. Cover with the lid and cook on low for
6—8 hours or until the pumpkin is tender.

When almost ready to serve, bring a large saucepan of
water to the boil, add the gnocchi, bring the water back
to the boil and cook for 2—3 minutes or until the
gnocchi float to the surface and are piping hot. Tip into
a colander to drain.

Stir the cream, then the gnocchi, into the pumpkin, mix
together lightly, then spoon into shallow bowls and
serve topped with grated Parmesan and a few extra
sage leaves, if liked.

For pumpkin pasta with dolcelatte, make up the
pumpkin mixture as above, then cook 250 g (8 oz)
rigatoni or penne pasta in a saucepan of boiling water
for 10 minutes or until tender. Drain. Stir the cream into
the pumpkin mixture as above, then stir in the pasta
instead of the gnocchi and top with 125 g (4 oz) diced
dolcelatte cheese instead of the Parmesan.

hot pickled beetroot

Preparation time **15 minutes**
Cooking temperature **low**
Cooking time **6–8 hours**
Serves **4**

1 tablespoon **olive oil**
2 **red onions**, roughly
   chopped
1 bunch of **beetroot**, about
   500 g (1 lb) in total,
   trimmed, peeled and cut into
   1.5 cm (½ inch) cubes
1 red-skinned **dessert apple**,
   cored and diced
4 cm (1½ inch) **fresh root
   ginger**, peeled and finely
   chopped
4 tablespoons **red wine
   vinegar**
2 tablespoons **clear honey**
450 ml (¾ pint) **vegetable
   stock**
salt and **pepper**

To garnish
soured cream
dill

Preheat the slow cooker if necessary; see the manufacturer's instructions. Heat the oil in a frying pan, add the onions and fry, stirring, for 5 minutes or until just beginning to soften and turn golden.

Stir in the beetroot and cook for 3 minutes, then add the apple, ginger, vinegar and honey. Pour in the stock, add a little salt and pepper and bring to the boil. Pour the mixture into the slow cooker pot, press the beetroot below the surface of the liquid then cover and cook on low for 6–8 hours until tender.

Serve hot as a starter topped with spoonfuls of soured cream and chopped dill or as a vegetable side dish with roast pork or beef or cold with cold sliced meats.

For hot beetroot with orange & caraway, make up the recipe as above but omit the ginger and vinegar, and instead add the grated rind and juice of 1 orange and 1½ teaspoons caraway seeds. Serve topped with spoonfuls of soured cream, a little paprika and some orange rind curls.

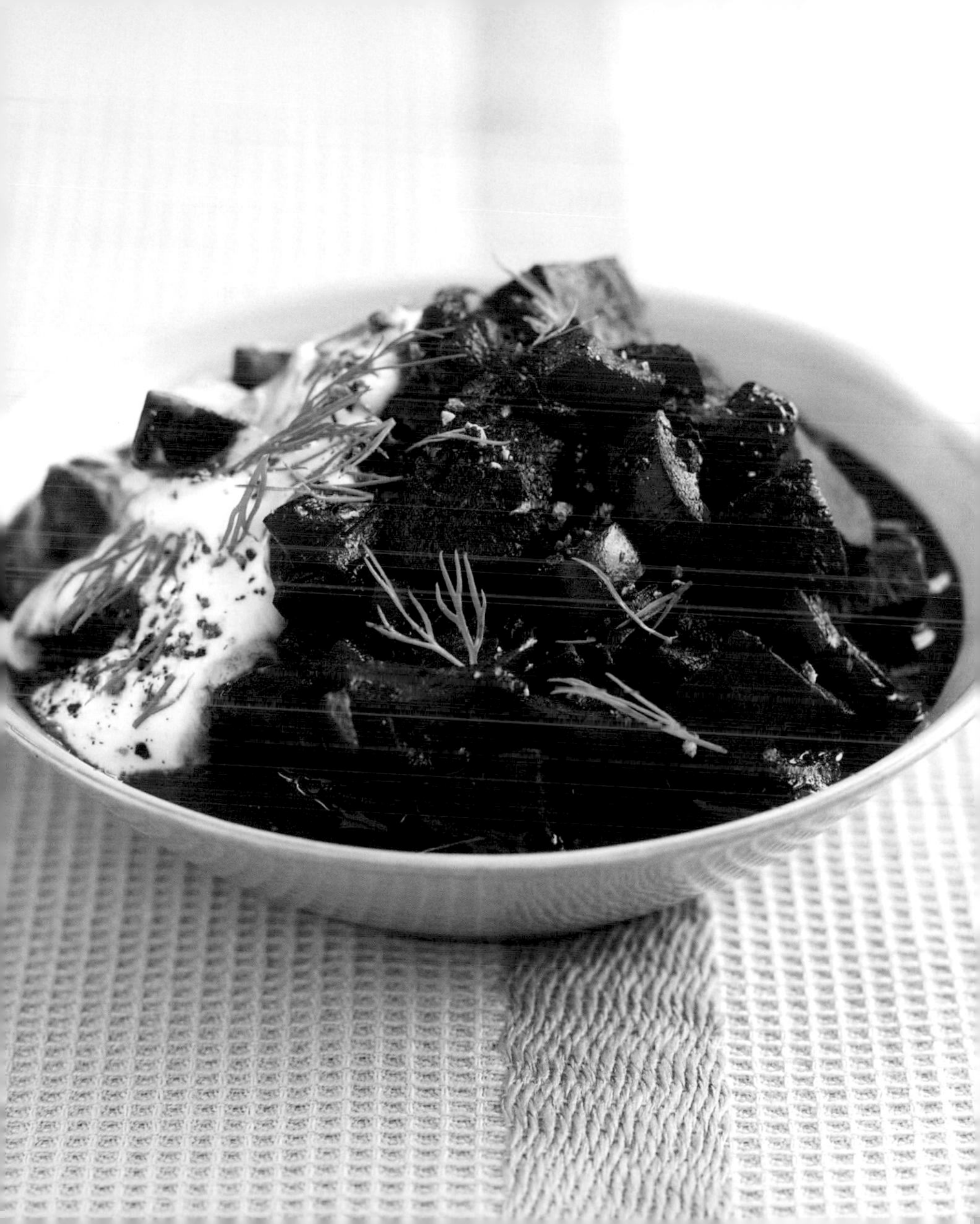

tarka dahl

Preparation time **15 minutes**
Cooking temperature **high**
Cooking time **3—4 hours**
Serves **4**

250 g (8 oz) **red lentils**
1 **onion**, finely chopped
½ teaspoon **turmeric**
½ teaspoon **cumin seeds**,
   roughly crushed
2 cm (¾ inch) **fresh root
   ginger**, peeled and finely
   chopped
200 g (7 oz) canned **chopped
   tomatoes**
600 ml (1 pint) boiling
   vegetable stock
salt and **pepper**
150 g (5 oz) **natural yogurt**
coriander leaves, torn,
   to garnish
warm **naan bread**, to serve

Tarka
1 tablespoon **sunflower oil**
2 teaspoons **black mustard
   seeds**
½ teaspoon **cumin seeds**,
   roughly crushed
pinch of **turmeric**
2 **garlic cloves**, finely
   chopped

Preheat the slow cooker if necessary; see the manufacturer's instructions. Rinse the lentils well with cold water, drain and put into the slow cooker pot with the onion, spices, ginger, tomatoes and boiling stock.

Stir in a little salt and pepper, cover with the lid and cook on high for 3—4 hours or until the lentils are soft and tender.

When almost ready to serve, make the tarka. Heat the oil in a small frying pan, add the remaining tarka ingredients and fry, stirring, for 2 minutes. Roughly mash the lentil mixture, then spoon into bowls, add spoonfuls of yogurt and drizzle with the tarka. Sprinkle with coriander leaves and serve with warm naan bread.

For tarka dahl with spinach, cook the lentils in the same way as above, adding 125 g (4 oz) washed and roughly shredded spinach leaves for the last 15 minutes. Fry the tarka spices as above, adding ¼ teaspoon crushed dried red chilli seeds, if liked.

spanish potatoes

Preparation time **15 minutes**
Cooking temperature **high**
Cooking time **4—5 hours**
Serves **4**

2 tablespoons **olive oil**
1 large **red onion**, thinly sliced
2 **garlic cloves**, finely
chopped
1 teaspoon **smoked paprika**
¼—½ teaspoon crushed dried
red chillies (to taste)
1 **red pepper**, cored,
deseeded and diced
1 **yellow pepper**, cored,
deseeded and diced
400 g (13 oz) can **chopped
tomatoes**
300 ml (½ pint) **vegetable
stock**
2—3 stems of **thyme**
50 g (2 oz) pitted **dry olives**
625 g (1¼ lb) **baking
potatoes**, cut into 2.5 cm
(1 inch) chunks
salt and **pepper**
crusty bread, to serve

Preheat the slow cooker if necessary; see the manufacturer's instructions. Heat the oil in a frying pan, add the onion and fry, stirring, for 5 minutes or until just beginning to turn golden.

Stir in the garlic, paprika, dried chillies and peppers and cook for 2 minutes. Mix in the tomatoes, stock, thyme, olives and some salt and pepper, then bring to the boil.

Add the potatoes to the slow cooker pot, pour over the hot tomato mixture, cover with the lid and cook on high for 4—5 hours or until the potatoes are tender. Serve with warm crusty bread and a dressed green salad, if liked.

For Spanish sweet potatoes, make up the recipe as above, using sweet potatoes instead of baking potatoes and omitting the olives. Cook on high for 3—4 hours and serve in bowls topped with spoonfuls of Greek yogurt and torn coriander leaves.

braised celery with orange

Preparation time **10 minutes**
Cooking temperature **high**
Cooking time **4—5 hours**
Serves **4—6**

2 **celery hearts**
grated rind and juice of
  1 small **orange**
2 tablespoons **light**
  muscovado sugar
400 g (13 oz) can **chopped**
  tomatoes
salt and **pepper**

Preheat the slow cooker if necessary; see the manufacturer's instructions. Cut each celery heart in half lengthways, then rinse under the cold tap to remove any traces of dirt. Drain and put into the slow cooker pot.

Mix the remaining ingredients together and pour over the celery. Cover with the lid and cook on high for 4—5 hours or until the celery is tender. If you would prefer a thicker sauce, pour off the liquid from the slow cooker pot into a saucepan and boil rapidly for 4—5 minutes to reduce. Pour back over the celery and serve as an accompaniment to roast chicken, pork or duck.

For braised fennel with orange, cut 3 small fennel bulbs into halves, add to the slow cooker pot with the remaining ingredients and cook as above. Sprinkle the top with 50 g (2 oz) torn ciabatta bread fried in 2 tablespoons olive oil until crisp and golden.

nut & apricot pilaf

Preparation time **25 minutes**
Cooking temperature **low**
Cooking time **3–3½ hours**
Serves **4**

1 tablespoon **olive oil**
1 large **onion**, chopped
75 g (3 oz) mixed **pistachios,
  walnuts** and **hazelnuts**
25 g (1 oz) **sunflower seeds**
200 g (7 oz) easy-cook **brown
  rice**
1 litre (1¾ pints) **vegetable
  stock**
75 g (3 oz) ready-to-eat dried
  apricots, chopped
25 g (1 oz) **currants**
1 **cinnamon stick**, halved
6 **cloves**
3 **bay leaves**
1 tablespoon **tomato purée**
salt and **pepper**
lightly toasted **mixed nuts**,
  to garnish

Preheat the slow cooker if necessary; see the manufacturer's instructions. Heat the oil in a frying pan, add the onion and fry, stirring, for 5 minutes or until lightly browned.

Add the nuts and seeds and fry until lightly browned. Stir in the rice and stock, followed by the dried fruit, spices, bay leaves and tomato purée, then season with salt and pepper to taste. Bring to the boil, stirring.

Transfer the mixture to the slow cooker pot. Cover with the lid and cook on low for 3–3½ hours or until the rice is tender and the stock has been absorbed. Discard the cinnamon, cloves and bay leaves before serving, garnished with extra nuts.

For aubergine & apricot pilaf, heat 3 tablespoons olive oil, add the onion and 1 sliced aubergine and fry until lightly browned. Continue as above, replacing the hazelnuts with almonds and adding the sunflower seeds, the rice, stock and just 50 g (2 oz) of the apricots plus 50 g (2 oz) chopped stoned dates. Add the remaining ingredients and continue as above.

desserts,
drinks &
preserves

sticky rum bananas with vanilla

Preparation time **10 minutes**
Cooking temperature **low**
Cooking time **1½–2 hours**
Serves **4**

25 g (1 oz) **butter**
75 g (3 oz) **light muscovado sugar**
grated rind and juice of 1 **lime**
1 **vanilla pod** or 1 teaspoon **vanilla extract**
3 tablespoons **white** or **dark rum**
200 ml (7 fl oz) boiling **water**
6 small **bananas**, peeled and halved lengthways
curls of **lime rind**, to decorate

Preheat the slow cooker if necessary; see the manufacturer's instructions. Add the butter, sugar and lime rind and juice to the warming slow cooker pot and stir until the butter has melted.

Slit the vanilla pod along its length, open it out with a small sharp knife and scrape the tiny black seeds away from inside the pod. Add the seeds and the pod or vanilla extract, if using, to the slow cooker pot along with the rum and boiling water.

Add the bananas to the slow cooker pot, arranging them in a single layer and pressing them beneath the liquid as much as you can. Cover with the lid and cook on low for 1½–2 hours or until the bananas are hot.

Spoon the bananas and rum sauce into dishes and decorate with extra lime rind curls and scoops of vanilla ice cream, if liked.

For sticky brandied pineapple, make up the vanilla syrup as above, replacing the rum with brandy. Trim the top off a medium pineapple, cut away the skin and eyes, and slice, then halve each slice, cutting away the core. Add to the syrup and press beneath the syrup. Cover and cook as above.

crème caramels

Preparation time **20 minutes**, plus chilling
Cooking temperature **low**
Cooking time **2½–3½ hours**
Serves **4**

butter, for greasing
125 g (4 oz) **granulated sugar**
125 ml (4 fl oz) **water**
2 tablespoons boiling **water**
2 **eggs**
3 **egg yolks**
400 g (13 oz) can **full-fat condensed milk**
125 ml (4 fl oz) **semi-skimmed milk**
grated rind of ½ small **lemon**

Preheat the slow cooker if necessary; see the manufacturer's instructions. Lightly butter 4 metal individual pudding moulds, each 250 ml (8 fl oz). Pour the sugar and water into a small saucepan and heat gently, stirring occasionally until the sugar has completely dissolved.

Increase the heat and boil the syrup for 5 minutes, without stirring, until the syrup has turned golden, keeping a watchful eye as it cooks. Take the pan off the heat, add the boiling water and stand well back. Tilt the pan to mix, and when bubbles have subsided pour into the pudding moulds, tilting them so that the syrup coats the base and sides.

Put the eggs and egg yolks into a bowl and fork together. Pour the condensed milk and fresh milk into a saucepan, bring to the boil, then gradually beat into the egg mixture until smooth. Strain back into the pan, then stir in the lemon rind.

Pour the custard into the syrup-lined pudding moulds, then transfer the moulds into the slow cooker pot. Cover the top of each one with a square of foil. Pour hot water around the moulds so that the water comes halfway up the sides, then cover with the lid and cook on low for 2½–3½ hours or until the custard is set with just a slight wobble in the centre. Lift out of the slow cooker pot with a tea towel, cool then transfer to the refrigerator for 3–4 hours or overnight to chill.

Dip the base of the moulds into boiling water for 10 seconds, loosen the top of the custard with a fingertip, then turn out on to rimmed plates.

saffron pears with chocolate

Preparation time **20 minutes**
Cooking temperature **low**
Cooking time **3–4 hours**
Serves **4**

300 ml (½ pint) cloudy **apple juice**
3 tablespoons **caster sugar**
large pinch of **saffron threads**
4 **cardamom pods**, roughly crushed
4 firm, ripe **pears**

Chocolate sauce
4 tablespoons **chocolate and hazelnut spread**
2 tablespoons **double cream**
2 tablespoons **milk**

Preheat the slow cooker if necessary; see the manufacturer's instructions. Pour the apple juice into a small saucepan, add the sugar, saffron and cardamom pods and their tiny black seeds. Bring to the boil, then tip into the slow cooker pot.

Cut each pear in half lengthways, leaving the stalk on, then cut away the skin. Remove the pear cores with a melon baller, if you have one, or a teaspoon. Add the pears to the slow cooker pot, pressing them beneath the surface of the liquid as much as you can. Cover with the lid and cook on low for 3–4 hours or until the pears are tender and pale yellow.

When ready to serve, put all the ingredients for the sauce into a small saucepan and warm together, stirring until smooth. Spoon the pears and some of the saffron sauce into shallow dishes, pour the chocolate sauce into a small jug and allow dinner guests to drizzle the sauce over the pears just before eating. Complete with a spoonful of ice cream or crème fraîche, if liked.

For spiced pears with red wine, warm 150 ml (¼ pint) red wine with 150 ml (¼ pint) water, 50 g (2 oz) caster sugar, the pared rind of ½ small orange, 1 small cinnamon stick, halved, and 4 cloves. Pour into the slow cooker pot, add 4 halved, peeled and cored pears, then cover and cook as above. Serve with spoonfuls of crème fraîche.

lemon custard creams

Preparation time **15 minutes**, plus chilling
Cooking temperature **low**
Cooking time **2–2½ hours**
Serves **6**

2 **eggs**
3 **egg yolks**
100 g (3½ oz) **caster sugar**
grated rind of 2 **lemons** and the juice of 1 **lemon**
300 ml (½ pint) **double cream**
150 g (5 oz) **blueberries**, to serve

Preheat the slow cooker if necessary; see the manufacturer's instructions. Put the eggs and egg yolks, sugar and lemon rind into a bowl and whisk together until just mixed.

Pour the cream into a small saucepan, bring just to the boil, then gradually whisk into the egg mixture. Strain the lemon juice and gradually whisk into the cream mixture.

Pour the mixture into 6 small coffee cups and put them in the slow cooker pot. Pour hot water into the pot so that it comes halfway up the sides of the cups. Loosely cover the tops of the cups with a piece of foil, cover and cook on low for 2–2½ hours or until the custards are just set.

Lift the cups carefully out of the slow cooker with a tea towel and leave to cool. Transfer to the refrigerator to chill for 3–4 hours or overnight.

Set the cups on their saucers and decorate the tops of the custard with blueberries.

For lime & elderflower custard creams, make the puddings as above but with the grated rind and juice of 2 limes and 2 tablespoons undiluted elderflower cordial instead of the lemon rind and juice. Cook in coffee cups, then serve chilled with fresh strawberries drizzled with a little extra elderflower cordial.

chocolate brownie puddings

Preparation time **20 minutes**
Cooking temperature **high**
Cooking time **1¼–1½ hours**
Serves **4**

125 g (4 oz) plain **dark
   chocolate**, plus 8 extra
   small squares
75 g (3 oz) **butter**
2 **eggs**
2 **egg yolks**
75 g (3 oz) **caster sugar**
½ teaspoon **vanilla extract**
40 g (1½ oz) **plain flour**

To decorate
sifted **icing sugar**
mini pastel-coloured
   marshmallows
vanilla ice cream or **crème
   fraîche**

Preheat the slow cooker if necessary; see the
manufacturer's instructions. Break the 125 g (4 oz)
chocolate into pieces, put into a saucepan with the
butter and heat gently, stirring occasionally, until melted.
Take off the heat and set aside.

Whisk together the whole eggs, egg yolks, sugar and
vanilla extract in a large bowl with an electric whisk for
3–4 minutes or until light and frothy. Gradually whisk in
the melted chocolate mixture.

Sift the flour into the chocolate mix and fold together.
Pour into 4 buttered and base-lined individual metal
pudding moulds, each 250 ml (8 fl oz). Press 2 squares
of chocolate into the centre of each, then loosely cover
the tops with squares of buttered foil.

Transfer the pudding moulds to the slow cooker pot
and pour boiling water into the pot to come halfway up
the sides of the moulds. Cover with the lid and cook on
high for 1¼–1½ hours until well risen and the tops
spring back when lightly pressed.

Loosen the puddings with a knife, turn out into shallow
serving dishes and remove the lining paper. Sprinkle
with sifted icing sugar. Serve with marshmallows,
spoonfuls of vanilla ice cream or crème fraîche.

For brandied cherry brownie puddings,
soak 8 drained canned pitted black cherries in
1 tablespoon of brandy for at least 2 hours, longer
if possible. Make up the brownie mixture as above
and drop 2 cherries into the centre of each instead
of the square of chocolate.

plum & polenta cake

Preparation time **30 minutes**
Cooking temperature **high**
Cooking time **3–3½ hours**
Serves **6**

150 g (5 oz) **butter**, at room
    temperature, plus extra for
    greasing
200 g (7 oz) sweet red
    plums, stoned and halved
150 g (5 oz) **caster sugar**
2 **eggs**, beaten
100 g (3½ oz) **ground
    almonds**
50 g (2 oz) fine **polenta**
    (cornmeal)
½ teaspoon **baking powder**
grated rind and juice of
    ½ **orange**

To decorate
2 tablespoons toasted **flaked
    almonds**
sifted **icing sugar**

Preheat the slow cooker if necessary; see the
manufacturer's instructions. Butter a 1.2 litre (2 pint)
oval or round heatproof dish that will fit comfortably in
your slow cooker pot and line the bottom with a piece
of greaseproof paper. Arrange the plum halves, cut side
down, in rings in the base of the dish.

Cream together the measured butter and sugar in a
mixing bowl until light and fluffy. Gradually beat the
eggs and ground almonds alternately into the mixture.
Stir in the polenta, baking powder and orange rind and
juice and beat until smooth.

Spoon the mixture over the plums and smooth with
a knife. Cover the dish with buttered foil, then stand it
on an upturned saucer or 2 individual flan rings in the
slow cooker pot. Pour boiling water into the pot to
come halfway up the sides of the dish. Cover and cook
on high for 3–3½ hours or until the top of the cake is
dry and springs back when pressed with a fingertip.

Remove the dish carefully from the slow cooker using
a tea towel. Take off the foil and leave to cool slightly.
Run a knife around the inside edge of the dish to
loosen the cake and turn it out on to a serving plate.
Remove the lining paper, sprinkle the top with toasted
flaked almonds and dust with a little sifted icing sugar
to decorate. Cut into wedges and serve warm or cold
with spoonfuls of whipped cream, if liked.

For apple & polenta cake, follow the recipe as
above, but replace the plums with 2 Braeburn dessert
apples, peeled, cored and thickly sliced and tossed
with the grated rind and juice of ½ lemon.

pineapple upside-down puddings

Preparation time **20 minutes**
Cooking temperature **high**
Cooking time **2–2½ hours**
Serves **4**

butter, for greasing
4 tablespoons **golden syrup**
2 tablespoons **light muscovado sugar**
220 g (7½ oz) can **pineapple rings**, drained, chopped
40 g (1½ oz) **glacé cherries**, roughly chopped

Sponge
50 g (2 oz) **butter**, at room temperature, or soft margarine
50 g (2 oz) **caster sugar**
50 g (2 oz) **self-raising flour**
25 g (1 oz) **desiccated coconut**
1 **egg**
1 tablespoon **milk**

Preheat the slow cooker if necessary; see the manufacturer's instructions. Lightly butter 4 metal individual pudding moulds, each 250 ml (8 fl oz), and base-line with a circle of nonstick baking paper. Add 1 tablespoon of golden syrup and ½ tablespoon sugar to the base of each, then add three-quarters of the pineapple and the cherries.

Make the sponge. Put all the ingredients plus the remaining pineapple into a bowl and beat together until smooth.

Spoon the mixture into the pudding moulds. Level the surface with the back of a small spoon, then cover the top of each mould loosely with buttered foil. Stand the moulds in the slow cooker pot, then pour boiling water into the pot to come halfway up the sides of the moulds. Cover with the lid and cook on high for 2–2½ hours or until the sponge is well risen and springs back when pressed with a fingertip.

Remove the foil, loosen the edges of the puddings with a round-bladed knife and turn out into shallow bowls. Peel away the lining paper and serve with hot custard, if liked.

For plum & almond puddings, add the syrup and sugar to the base of the moulds as above, then add 4 stoned and sliced red plums instead of the pineapple and cherries. Make up the sponge as above, omitting the coconut and adding 25 g (1 oz) ground almonds and a few drops of almond essence.

chocolate bread & butter pudding

Preparation time **35 minutes**
Cooking temperature **low**
Cooking time **4–4½ hours**
Serves **4–5**

½ **French stick**, thinly sliced
50 g (2 oz) **butter**, at room
  temperature
100 g (3½ oz) **white
  chocolate**, chopped
4 **egg yolks**
50 g (2 oz) **caster sugar**, plus
  3 tablespoons extra for
  caramelizing
150 ml (¼ pint) **double
  cream**
300 ml (½ pint) **milk**
1 teaspoon **vanilla extract**

Blueberry coulis
125 g (4 oz) **blueberries**
1 tablespoon **caster sugar**
4 tablespoons **water**

To decorate
few extra **blueberries**
little **white chocolate**,
  chopped

Preheat the slow cooker if necessary; see the manufacturer's instructions. Spread the slices of French bread with the butter. Layer the bread in a 1.2 litre (2 pint) heatproof dish that will fit comfortably in your slow cooker pot, allowing for a gap of at least 1.5 cm (¾ inch) all the way around. Sprinkle the chopped white chocolate between the layers of bread.

Beat together the egg yolks and sugar in a bowl with a fork. Pour the cream and milk into a saucepan and bring just to the boil. Gradually stir into the egg mixture, then stir in the vanilla extract.

Pour the cream mixture over the layered bread slices and leave to stand for 10 minutes.

Cover the top of the dish with foil, then lower it into the slow cooker pot, using foil straps or a string pudding bowl lifter (see page 15). Pour hot water around the dish to come halfway up the sides, cover with the lid and cook on low for 4–4½ hours or until the custard has set.

Meanwhile, make the blueberry coulis. Purée the blueberries with the sugar and water until smooth. Pour into a jug and set aside.

Lift the dish carefully out of the slow cooker. Remove the foil and sprinkle the remaining sugar over the top of the pudding. Caramelize the sugar under a hot grill or with a cook's blowtorch. To serve, spoon the bread and butter pudding into bowls and sprinkle with extra blueberries and white chocolate. Stir the blueberry coulis and pour it around the pudding.

lemon & poppy seed drizzle cake

Preparation time **25 minutes**
Cooking temperature **high**
Cooking time **4½—5 hours**
Serves **6—8**

125 g (4 oz) **butter**, at room
temperature, plus extra
for greasing
125 g (4 oz) **caster sugar**
2 **eggs**, beaten
125 g (4 oz) **self-raising flour**
2 tablespoons **poppy seeds**
grated rind of 1 **lemon**
lemon rind curls, to decorate
crème fraîche, to serve

Lemon syrup
juice of 1½ **lemons**
125 g (4 oz) **caster sugar**

Preheat the slow cooker if necessary; see the manufacturer's instructions. Lightly butter a soufflé dish that is 14 cm (5½ inches) across the base and 9 cm (3½ inches) high, and base-line with a circle of nonstick baking paper.

Cream together the measured butter and sugar in a bowl with a wooden spoon or electric hand mixer. Gradually mix in alternate spoonfuls of beaten egg and flour, and continue adding and beating until the mixture is smooth. Stir in the poppy seeds and lemon rind, then spoon the mixture into the soufflé dish and spread the top level. Cover the top of the dish loosely with buttered foil and then lower into the slow cooker pot using foil straps (see page 15).

Pour boiling water into the slow cooker pot so that it comes halfway up the sides of the dish. Cover with the lid and cook on high for 4½—5 hours or until the cake is dry and springs back when pressed with a fingertip.

Lift the dish carefully out of the slow cooker, remove the foil and loosen the edge of the cake with a knife. Turn out on to a plate or shallow dish with a rim. Quickly warm the lemon juice and sugar together for the syrup and as soon as the sugar has dissolved, pour the syrup over the cake. Leave to cool and for the syrup to soak in. Cut into slices and serve with spoonfuls of crème fraîche, decorated with lemon rind curls.

For citrus drizzle cake, omit the lemon rind and poppy seeds from the cake mixture and stir in the grated rind of ½ lemon, ½ lime and ½ small orange. Bake as above. Make the syrup using the juice of grated fruits and sugar.

sticky toffee apple pudding

Preparation time **30 minutes**
Cooking temperature **high**
Cooking time **3–3½ hours**
Serves **4–5**

50 g (2 oz) **butter**, diced, plus
extra for greasing
150 g (5 oz) **self-raising flour**
100 g (3½ oz) **dark muscovado sugar**
2 **eggs**
2 tablespoons **milk**
1 **dessert apple**, cored and
finely chopped
vanilla ice cream, **crème fraîche** or **pouring cream**,
to serve

Sauce
125 g (4 oz) **dark muscovado sugar**
25 g (1 oz) **butter**, diced
300 ml (½ pint) boiling **water**

Preheat the slow cooker if necessary; see the manufacturer's instructions. Butter the inside of a soufflé dish that is 14 cm (5½ inches) across and 9 cm (3½ inches) high. Put the flour in a bowl, add the measured butter and rub in with the fingertips until the mixture resembles fine breadcrumbs. Stir in the sugar, then mix in the eggs and milk until smooth. Stir in the apple.

Spoon the mixture into the soufflé dish and spread it level. Sprinkle the sugar for the sauce over the top and dot with the 25 g (1 oz) butter. Pour the measured boiling water over the top, then cover loosely with foil.

Lower the dish carefully into the slow cooker pot using a string handle or foil straps (see page 15). Pour boiling water into the pot so that it comes halfway up the sides of the soufflé dish. Cover and cook on high for 3–3½ hours or until the sponge is well risen and the sauce is bubbling around the edges.

Lift the dish out of the slow cooker. Remove the foil and loosen the sides of the sponge. Cover with a dish that is large enough to catch the sauce, then invert and remove the soufflé dish. Serve with spoonfuls of vanilla ice cream, crème fraîche or pouring cream.

For sticky banana pudding, prepare the pudding as above but replace the chopped apple with 1 small, ripe and roughly mashed banana and ½ teaspoon ground cinnamon. Make up the sauce and cook as above.

iced jamaican ginger cake

Preparation time **25 minutes**
Cooking temperature **high**
Cooking time **4½–5 hours**
Serves **6**

100 g (3½ oz) **butter**, plus
  extra for greasing
100 g (3½ oz) **dark**
  muscovado sugar
100 g (3½ oz) **golden syrup**
100 g (3½ oz) ready-chopped
  stoned **dates**
100 g (3½ oz) **wholemeal**
  plain flour
100 g (3½ oz) **self-raising**
  flour
½ teaspoon **bicarbonate of**
  soda
2 teaspoons **ground ginger**
3 pieces of **stem ginger**,
  drained of syrup, 2 chopped
  and 1 cut into strips
2 **eggs**, beaten
100 ml (3½ fl oz) **milk**
125 g (4 oz) **icing sugar**
3–3½ teaspoons **water**

Preheat the slow cooker if necessary; see the manufacturer's instructions. Butter a soufflé dish that is 14 cm (5½ inches) across the base and 9 cm (3½ inches) high and base-line with a circle of nonstick baking paper.

Put the measured butter, sugar, syrup and dates into a saucepan and heat gently, stirring, until the butter and sugar have melted. Take the pan off the heat, add the flours, bicarbonate of soda, ground and chopped ginger, eggs and milk and beat until smooth. Pour into the lined dish and cover the top loosely with buttered foil.

Lower the dish carefully into the slow cooker pot on foil straps (see page 15) or tie string around the top edge of the dish. Pour boiling water into the pot to come halfway up the sides of the dish, cover with the lid and cook on high for 4½–5 hours or until a skewer comes out cleanly when inserted into the centre of the ginger cake.

Take the dish out of the slow cooker pot, leave to stand for 10 minutes, then remove the foil and loosen the edge of the cake with a knife. Turn out on to a wire rack, peel off the lining paper and leave to cool.

Sift the icing sugar into a bowl and mix in just enough water to make a smooth, thick icing. Spoon over the top of the cake, then decorate with the strips of ginger. Leave to set. Cut into wedges to serve.

For banana ginger cake, omit the dates from the ginger cake and add 1 small mashed banana mixed with 1 tablespoon lemon juice when adding the chopped ginger. Cook and ice as above.

cherry & chocolate puddings

Preparation time **25 minutes**
Cooking temperature **high**
Cooking time **1½–2 hours**
Serves **4**

50 g (2 oz) **butter**, plus extra
  for greasing
50 g (2 oz) **caster sugar**
50 g (2 oz) **self-raising flour**
1 **egg**
1 tablespoon **cocoa powder**
¼ teaspoon **baking powder**
¼ teaspoon **ground**
  cinnamon
425 g (14 oz) can pitted **black**
  cherries, drained

Chocolate sauce
100 g (3½ oz) **white**
  chocolate, broken into
  pieces
150 ml (¼ pint) **double**
  cream

Preheat the slow cooker if necessary; see the manufacturer's instructions. Butter the inside of 4 metal pudding moulds, each 250 ml (8 fl oz), and base-line each with a circle of greaseproof paper.

Put the measured butter, sugar, flour, egg, cocoa, baking powder and cinnamon in a bowl and beat them together with a wooden spoon until smooth.

Arrange 7 cherries in the base of each pudding mould. Roughly chop the remainder and stir them into the pudding mix. Spoon the mixture into the pudding moulds and level the tops. Loosely cover the tops of the moulds with foil and put them in the slow cooker pot. Pour boiling water into the pot so that it comes halfway up the sides of the moulds, cover with the lid and cook on high for 1½–2 hours or until the puddings are well risen and the tops spring back when pressed with a fingertip. Lift the puddings out of the slow cooker pot.

Make the sauce. Put the chocolate and cream in a small saucepan and heat gently, stirring occasionally, until melted. Loosen the edges of the puddings, turn them out into shallow bowls, peel away the lining paper and pour the sauce around them before serving.

For cherry & almond puddings, prepare the sponge as above, omitting the cocoa and ground cinnamon and instead adding 2 tablespoons ground almonds and a few drops of almond essence. Cook as above, turn out and serve with spoonfuls of vanilla ice cream.

dark chocolate & coffee pots

Preparation time **25 minutes**, plus chilling
Cooking temperature **low**
Cooking time **3–3½ hours**
Serves **4**

450 ml (¾ pint) **full-fat milk**
150 ml (¼ pint) **double cream**
200 g (7 oz) plain **dark chocolate**, broken into pieces
2 **eggs**
3 **egg yolks**
50 g (2 oz) **caster sugar**
¼ teaspoon **ground cinnamon**
chocolate curls, to decorate

Topping
150 ml (¼ pint) **double cream**
75 ml (3 fl oz) **coffee cream liqueur**

Preheat the slow cooker if necessary; see the manufacturer's instructions. Pour the milk and cream into a saucepan and bring just to the boil. Remove from the heat, add the chocolate pieces and set aside for 5 minutes, stirring occasionally, until the chocolate has melted.

Put the whole eggs, egg yolks, sugar and cinnamon in a mixing bowl and whisk until smooth. Gradually whisk in the warm chocolate milk, then strain the mixture into 4 heatproof pots or mugs, each 250 ml (8 fl oz).

Cover the tops of the pots or mugs with foil and stand them in the slow cooker pot. Pour hot water into the slow cooker pot to come halfway up the sides of the pots or mugs. Cover with the lid and cook on low for 3–3½ hours or until set.

Lift the dishes carefully out of the slow cooker pot using oven gloves. Leave to cool at room temperature, then transfer to the refrigerator for at least 4 hours until well chilled.

Just before serving, whip the cream for the topping until soft swirls form. Gradually whisk in the liqueur, then spoon the flavoured cream over the top of the desserts. Sprinkle with chocolate curls and serve.

For cappuccino pots with coffee cream liqueur, add 2 teaspoons instant coffee to the just-boiled cream and milk when adding the chocolate. Continue as above, but omit the cinnamon.

peaches with marsala & vanilla

Preparation time **15 minutes**
Cooking temperature **low** and **high**
Cooking time **1¼–1¾ hours**
Serves **4–6**

150 ml (¼ pint) **Marsala** or **sweet sherry**
150 ml (¼ pint) **water**
75 g (3 oz) **caster sugar**
6 firm, ripe **peaches** or **nectarines**, halved and stones removed
1 **vanilla pod**, slit lengthways
2 teaspoons **cornflour**
125 g (4 oz) **raspberries**

Preheat the slow cooker if necessary; see the manufacturer's instructions. Put the Marsala or sherry, the water and sugar in a saucepan and bring to the boil.

Put the peach or nectarine halves and vanilla pod in the slow cooker pot and pour in the hot syrup. Cover with the lid and cook on low for 1–1½ hours or until hot and tender.

Lift the fruit out of the slow cooker pot and transfer to a serving dish. Remove the vanilla pod, then scrape the black seeds from the pod with a small sharp knife and stir the seeds back into the cooking syrup. Mix the cornflour to a smooth paste with a little cold water, then stir into the cooking syrup and cook on high for 15 minutes, stirring occasionally.

Pour the thickened syrup over the fruit, sprinkle with the raspberries and serve warm or chilled with spoonfuls of crème fraîche or vanilla ice cream, if liked.

For poached apples & pears with Marsala & vanilla, make the Marsala syrup as above. Peel, core and quarter 3 Braeburn dessert apples and 3 just-ripe pears. Add the fruit to the slow cooker pot with a slit vanilla pod and pour over the hot syrup. Cook and thicken the syrup as above.

christmas pudding

Preparation time **20 minutes**
Cooking temperature **high**
Cooking time **7–8 hours**
Reheating time **2–2½ hours**
Serves **6–8**

butter, for greasing
750 g (1½ lb) mixed luxury
    dried fruit (with larger fruits
    diced)
50 g (2 oz) **pistachio nuts**,
    roughly chopped
25 g (1 oz) glacé or stem
    ginger, finely chopped
1 **dessert apple**, peeled,
    cored and coarsely grated
grated rind and juice of
    1 **lemon**
grated rind and juice of
    1 **orange**
4 tablespoons **brandy**
50 g (2 oz) soft **dark
    muscovado sugar**
50 g (2 oz) **self-raising flour**
75 g (3 oz) **breadcrumbs**
100 g (3½ oz) **vegetable
    suet**
1 teaspoon **ground mixed
    spice**
2 **eggs**, beaten
4 tablespoons **brandy**,
    to serve (optional)

Preheat the slow cooker if necessary; see the manufacturer's instructions. Check that a 1.5 litre (2½ pint) pudding basin will fit inside your slow cooker pot with a little room to spare, then butter the inside of the basin and base-line with a circle of nonstick baking paper.

Put the dried fruit, nuts, ginger and grated apple into a large bowl. Add the fruit rinds and juice and brandy and mix together well. Stir in the remaining ingredients. Spoon into the buttered basin, pressing down well as you go. Cover with a large circle of nonstick baking paper, then a piece of foil. Tie with string and add a string handle.

Lower into the slow cooker pot, using foil straps (see page 15) and pour boiling water into the pot to come two-thirds up the sides of the basin. Cover with the lid and cook on high for 7–8 hours. Check halfway through cooking and top up with extra boiling water if needed. Take out of the slow cooker and leave to cool.

Cover with fresh foil, leaving the baking paper in place. Retie with string and keep in a cool place for 2 months or until Christmas.

When ready to serve, preheat the slow cooker if needed, add the pudding and boiling water as above and reheat on high for 2–2½ hours. Remove the foil and paper, loosen the pudding and turn out. Warm the brandy in a saucepan, if using. When it is just boiling, flame with a taper and quickly pour over the pudding. Serve with brandy butter or cream.

winter fruit compote

Preparation time **10 minutes**
Cooking temperature **low**
Cooking time **2½–3½ hours**
Serves **4**

300 g (10 oz) **cranberries**
500 g (1 lb) red **plums**,
 quartered and stoned
200 g (7 oz) red seedless
 grapes, halved
4 teaspoons **cornflour**
300 ml (½ pint) red **grape
 juice**
100 g (3½ oz) **caster sugar**
1 **cinnamon stick**, halved
pared rind of 1 small **orange**

Lemon curd cream
150 ml (¼ pint) **double
 cream**, lightly whipped
3 tablespoons **lemon curd**

Preheat the slow cooker if necessary; see the manufacturer's instructions. Put the cranberries, plums and grapes into the slow cooker pot.

Mix the cornflour with a little of the grape juice in a bowl until smooth, then stir in the remaining juice. Pour into the slow cooker pot and add the sugar, cinnamon and orange rind. Stir together, then cover with the lid and cook on low for 2½–3½ hours or until the fruit is tender.

Stir, discard the cinnamon and orange rind and serve warm or cold spooned into bowls and topped with the cream folded into the lemon curd.

For orchard fruit compote, follow the recipe as above, but replace the cranberries and grapes with 2 pears and 2 dessert apples, peeled, cored and thickly sliced.

baked apples with dates

Preparation time **20 minutes**
Cooking temperature **low**
Cooking time **3–4 hours**
Serves **4**

50 g (2 oz) **butter**, at room
  temperature
50 g (2 oz) **light muscovado
  sugar**
½ teaspoon **ground
  cinnamon**
grated rind of ½ small orange
1 tablespoon finely chopped
  glacé or drained **stem
  ginger**
50 g (2 oz) ready-chopped
  stoned **dates**
4 large Braeburn or other firm
  dessert apples
150 ml (¼ pint) cloudy **apple
  juice**
hot **custard** or **cream** to serve

Preheat the slow cooker if necessary; see the manufacturer's instructions. Mix together the butter, sugar, cinnamon and orange rind until smooth, then stir in the chopped ginger and dates.

Trim a thin slice off the bottom of the apples, if needed, so that they will stand up without rolling over, then cut a thick slice off the top of each and reserve for later. Using a small knife, cut away the apple core to leave a cavity for the stuffing.

Divide the date mixture into 4 and press a portion into each apple cavity, spreading it over the top cut edge of the apple if it won't all fit in. Replace the apple lids and then put the apples into the slow cooker pot. Pour the apple juice into the base of the pot, cover with the lid and cook on low for 3–4 hours or until the apples are tender.

Lift the apples carefully out of the slow cooker and serve in shallow dishes with the sauce spooned over and a drizzle of hot custard or cream.

For baked apples with gingered cherries, follow the recipe as above, but omit the cinnamon, replace the orange rind with lemon rind and replace the dates with 50 g (2 oz) chopped glacé cherries.

compote with mascarpone

Preparation time **20 minutes**
Cooking temperature **high**
Cooking time **1–1¼ hours**
Serves **4**

4 **nectarines**, halved, stoned
  and flesh diced
250 g (8 oz) **strawberries**,
  halved or quartered
  depending on size
50 g (2 oz) **caster sugar**, plus
  2 tablespoons
finely grated rind and juice of
  2 **oranges**
125 ml (4 fl oz) cold **water**
150 g (5 oz) **mascarpone**
  cheese
40 g (1½ oz) **amaretti**
  biscuits

Preheat the slow cooker if necessary; see the manufacturer's instructions. Put the nectarines and strawberries in the slow cooker pot with 50 g (2 oz) sugar, the rind of 1 orange, the juice of 1½ oranges and the measured water. Cover and cook on high for 1–1¼ hours or until the fruit is tender. Serve warm or cold.

Just before the compote is ready, mix the mascarpone with the remaining sugar, orange rind and juice. Reserve some of the amaretti biscuits for decoration. Crumble the rest with your fingertips into the bowl with the mascarpone and stir until mixed. Spoon the fruit into tumblers, top with spoonfuls of the orange mascarpone mixture and decorate with a sprinkling of amaretti biscuit crumbs.

For plum & cranberry compote with orange mascarpone, replace the nectarines and strawberries with 625g (1¼ lb) plums, quartered and stoned, and 125 g (4 oz) cranberries (no need to thaw if frozen). Increase the sugar to 75 g (3 oz), then follow the recipe above, using cranberry and raspberry juice instead of water, if liked.

blackberry & apple jam

Preparation time **20 minutes**
Cooking temperature **high**
Cooking time **4–5 hours**
Makes **4 × 400 g (13 oz) jars**

1 kg (2 lb) **cooking apples**,
  peeled, cored and chopped
500 g (1 lb) **granulated
  sugar**
grated rind of **1 lemon**
2 tablespoons **water** or **lemon
  juice**
250 g (8 oz) **blackberries**

Preheat the slow cooker if necessary; see the manufacturer's instructions. Put all the ingredients in the slow cooker pot, in the order listed. Cover with the lid and cook on high for 4–5 hours, stirring once or twice during cooking. By the end of the cooking time the fruit should be thick and pulpy.

Warm 4 clean jars in the bottom of a low oven. Spoon in the jam, place a waxed disc on top and leave to cool. Seal each jar with a cellophane jam pot cover and an elastic band, label and store for up to 2 months in the refrigerator. (The jam's low sugar content means that it does not keep as long as conventional jam and must be kept in the refrigerator.)

For apple, plum & mixed berry jam, replace half the apples with 500 g (1 lb) stoned and chopped red plums and half the blackberries with 125 g (4 oz) raspberries. Cook and store as above.

tangy citrus curd

Preparation time **25 minutes**
Cooking temperature **low**
Cooking time **3–4 hours**
Makes **2 × 400 g (13 oz) jars**

125 g (4 oz) **unsalted butter**
400 g (13 oz) **caster sugar**
grated rind and juice of
  2 **lemons**
grated rind and juice of
  1 **orange**
grated rind and juice of 1 **lime**
4 **eggs**, beaten

Preheat the slow cooker if necessary; see the manufacturer's instructions. Put the butter and sugar in a saucepan, add the fruit rinds, then strain in the juice. Heat gently for 2–3 minutes, stirring occasionally, until the butter has melted and the sugar has dissolved.

Pour the mixture into a basin that will fit comfortably in your slow cooker pot. Leave to cool for 10 minutes, then gradually strain in the eggs and mix well. Cover the basin with foil, put foil straps or a string pudding bowl lifter (see page 15) in the slow cooker pot and place the basin on top. Pour hot water into the cooker pot to come halfway up the sides of the basin. Cover with the lid and cook on low for 3–4 hours or until the mixture is very thick. Stir once or twice during cooking if possible.

Warm 2 clean jars in the bottom of a low oven. Spoon in the citrus curd, place a waxed disc on top and leave to cool. Seal each jar with a screw-top lid or a cellophane jam pot cover and an elastic band, label and store in the refrigerator. Use within 3–4 weeks.

For lemon curd, prepare as above, but omit the orange and lime and use 3 lemons, rather than 2. Cook and store as above.

chillied tomato & garlic chutney

Preparation time **30 minutes**
Cooking temperature **high**
Cooking time **6–8 hours**
Makes **5 × 400 g (13 oz) jars**

1 kg (2 lb) **tomatoes**, skinned
   and roughly chopped
1 large **onion**, chopped
2 **cooking apples**, about
   500 g (1 lb), peeled, cored
   and chopped
2 **red peppers**, cored,
   deseeded and diced
75 g (3 oz) **sultanas**
100 ml (3½ fl oz) distilled
   malt vinegar
250 g (8 oz) **granulated
   sugar**
2–3 large mild **red chillies**,
   halved, deseeded and finely
   chopped
6–8 **garlic cloves**, finely
   chopped
1 **cinnamon stick**, halved
½ teaspoon **ground allspice**
1 teaspoon **salt**
pepper

Preheat the slow cooker if necessary; see the manufacturer's instructions. Put all the ingredients in the slow cooker pot and mix together. Cover with the lid and cook on high for 6–8 hours or until thick and pulpy, stirring once or twice.

Warm 5 clean jars in the bottom of a low oven. Spoon in the chutney, place a waxed disc on top and leave to cool. Seal each jar with a screw-topped lid, then label. Store in a cool place for up to 2 months. Once opened, store in the refrigerator.

For spiced green tomato chutney, replace the tomatoes with 1 kg (2 lb) green tomatoes (chopped but not skinned) and replace the onion and peppers with 3 onions weighing 500 g (1 lb) in total. Mix the tomatoes and onions with the cooking apples, vinegar, sugar, chillies and salt. Decrease the garlic cloves to 2 and replace the cinnamon and allspice with 1 teaspoon ground ginger, 1 teaspoon turmeric and 1 teaspoon roughly crushed cloves. Cook and store as above.

pickled plums

Preparation time **20 minutes**
Cooking temperature **high**
Cooking time **2–2½ hours**
Makes **2** × 750 ml (1¼ pint)
   jars and **1** × 500 ml
   (17 fl oz) le parfait jar

750 ml (1¼ pints) **white wine vinegar**
500 g (1 lb) **caster sugar**
7 sprigs of **rosemary**
7 sprigs of **thyme**
7 small **bay leaves**
4 sprigs of **lavender** (optional)
4 **garlic cloves**, unpeeled
1 teaspoon **salt**
½ teaspoon **peppercorns**
1.5 kg (3 lb) firm red **plums**, washed and pricked

Preheat the slow cooker if necessary; see the manufacturer's instructions. Pour the vinegar and sugar into the slow cooker pot, then add 4 sprigs each of the rosemary and thyme and the bay leaves, all the lavender (if used), the garlic cloves, salt and peppercorns. Cover with the lid and cook on high for 2–2½ hours, stirring once or twice.

Warm the 3 clean jars in the bottom of a low oven. Pack the plums tightly into the jars. Tuck the remaining fresh herbs into the jars. Strain in the hot vinegar, making sure that the plums are completely covered, then seal tightly with rubber seals and jar lids.

Label the jars and leave to cool. Transfer to a cool, dark cupboard and store for 3–4 weeks before using. Once opened, store in the refrigerator.

For pickled shallots, trim a little off the tops and roots of 1.25 kg (2½ lb) small shallots. Put them in a bowl and cover with boiling water, leave to soak for 3 minutes, then pour off the water and re-cover with cold water. Lift the shallots out one at a time and peel off the brown skins. Drain and layer in a second bowl with 40 g (1½ oz) salt. Leave overnight. Make up the vinegar mixture in the slow cooker as above, but using 250 g (8 oz) caster sugar and 250 g (8 oz) light muscovado sugar and omitting the lavender. Tip the shallots into a colander and drain off as much liquid as possible. Rinse with cold water, drain and pat dry with kitchen paper. Pack tightly into warmed jars, adding a few extra herbs. Pour over the hot, strained vinegar, add crumpled greaseproof paper to keep the shallots beneath the surface of the vinegar, and finish as above.

hot mexican coffee

Preparation time **10 minutes**
Cooking temperature **low**
Cooking time **3–4 hours**
Serves **4**

50 g (2 oz) **cocoa powder**
4 teaspoons **instant coffee granules**
1 litre (1¾ pints) boiling **water**
150 ml (¼ pint) **dark rum**
100 g (3½ oz) **caster sugar**
½ teaspoon **ground cinnamon**
1 large dried or fresh **red chilli**, halved
150 ml (¼) pint **double cream**

To decorate
2 tablespoons grated plain **dark chocolate**

Preheat the slow cooker if necessary; see the manufacturer's instructions. Put the cocoa and instant coffee in a bowl and mix to a smooth paste with a little of the boiling water.

Pour the cocoa paste into the slow cooker pot. Add the remaining boiling water, the rum, sugar, cinnamon and red chilli and mix together. Cover with the lid and cook on low for 3–4 hours until piping hot or until the coffee is required.

Stir well, then ladle into heatproof glasses. Whip the cream until it is just beginning to hold its shape and spoon a little into each glass. Decorate each drink with a little grated chocolate and a dried chilli, if liked.

For hot mocha coffee, reduce the amount of boiling water to 900 ml (1½ pints) and use 1 teaspoon vanilla extract instead of the rum and chilli. Cook as above, then whisk in 300 ml (½ pint) milk. Pour into heatproof glasses, top with cream as above and decorate with a few mini marshmallows.

lemon cordial

Preparation time **10 minutes**

Cooking temperature **high** and **low**

Cooking time **3–4 hours**

Makes about **20 glasses**

3 **lemons**, washed and thinly sliced

625 g (1¼ lb) **granulated sugar**

900 ml (1½ pints) boiling **water**

25 g (1 oz) **tartaric acid**

Preheat the slow cooker if necessary; see the manufacturer's instructions. Add the lemon slices to the slow cooker pot with the sugar and boiling water and stir well until the sugar is almost all dissolved. Cover with the lid and cook on high for 1 hour.

Reduce the heat and cook on low for 2–3 hours or until the lemons are almost translucent. Switch off the slow cooker and stir in the tartaric acid. Leave to cool.

Remove and discard some of the sliced lemons using a slotted spoon. Transfer the cordial and remaining lemon slices to 2 sterilized screw-topped, wide-necked bottles or storage jars. Seal well, label and store in the refrigerator for up to 1 month.

Dilute the cordial with water in a ratio of 1:3, adding a few of the sliced lemons for decoration, ice cubes and sprigs of fresh mint or lemon balm, if liked.

For lemon & lime cordial, prepare the cordial using 2 lemons and 2 limes, washed and thinly sliced (instead of 3 lemons). Serve diluted with sparkling mineral water and sprigs of mint.

hot jamaican punch

Preparation time **10 minutes**
Cooking temperature **high** and **low**
Cooking time **3–4 hours**
Serves **6**

juice of 3 **limes**
300 ml (½ pint) **dark rum**
300 ml (½ pint) **ginger wine**
600 ml (1 pint) cold **water**
75 g (3 oz) **caster sugar**

To decorate
1 **lime**, thinly sliced
2 slices of **pineapple**, cored but skin left on and cut into pieces

Preheat the slow cooker if necessary; see the manufacturer's instructions. Strain the lime juice into the slow cooker pot and discard the pips. Add the rum, ginger wine, water and sugar, cover and cook on high for 1 hour.

Reduce the heat to low and cook for 2–3 hours until the punch is piping hot or until you are ready to serve. Stir well, then ladle into heatproof glasses and add a slice of lime and 2 pieces of pineapple to each glass.

For rum toddy, put the grated rind of 1 lemon and 1 orange and the juice of 3 lemons and 3 oranges into the slow cooker. Add 125 g (4 oz) set honey and the sugar. Increase the water to 750 ml (1¼ pints) and reduce the rum to 150 ml (¼ pint). Cook and serve as above.

mulled cranberry & red wine

Preparation time **10 minutes**
Cooking temperature **high** and **low**
Cooking time **4–5 hours**
Makes **8–10 glasses**

75 cl bottle inexpensive **red wine**
600 ml (1 pint) **cranberry juice**
100 ml (3½ fl oz) **brandy, rum, vodka** or **orange liqueur**
100 g (3½ oz) **caster sugar**
1 **orange**
8 **cloves**
1–2 **cinnamon sticks** (depending on size)

To serve
1 **orange**, cut into segments
2–3 **bay leaves**
few fresh **cranberries**

Preheat the slow cooker if necessary; see the manufacturer's instructions. Pour the red wine, cranberry juice and brandy or other alcohol into the slow cooker pot. Stir in the sugar.

Stud the orange segments with a clove. Break the cinnamon sticks into large pieces and add to the pot with the orange pieces. Cover with the lid and cook on high for 1 hour. Reduce the temperature and cook on low for 3–4 hours.

Replace the orange segments with new ones and add the bay leaves and cranberries. Ladle into heatproof glasses, keeping back the fruits and herbs, if liked.

For mulled orange & red wine, prepare the wine as above, but omit the cranberry juice and instead add 300 ml (½ pint) orange juice from a carton and 300 ml (½ pint) water. Serve decorated with extra herbs and fruit.

index

acknowledgements

Executive Editor Eleanor Maxfield
Senior Editor Charlotte Macey
Executive Art Editor Karen Sawyer
Designer Mark Stevens
Photographer Stephen Conroy
Home Economist Sara Lewis
Props Stylist Liz Hippisley
Production Controller Carolin Stransky

Commissioned Photography © Octopus Publishing Group Ltd/Stephen Conroy